Human choice
and climate change

Human choice and climate change

EDITED BY
Steve Rayner & Elizabeth L. Malone

VOLUME ONE
The societal framework

VOLUME TWO
Resources and technology

VOLUME THREE
The tools for policy analysis

VOLUME FOUR
"What have we learned?"

Human choice and climate change

VOLUME FOUR
"What have we learned?"

EDITED BY

Steve Rayner
Elizabeth L. Malone

Pacific Northwest National Laboratory

Battelle Press

DISCLAIMER

Funding for the publication of this volume and funding for a portion of the research discussed in this volume were provided by the United States Department of Energy (DOE). The views and opinions of the authors expressed herein do not necessarily state or reflect those of the DOE. Neither the DOE, nor Battelle Memorial Institute, nor any of their employees, makes any warranty, expressed or implied, or assumes any legal liability or responsibility for the accuracy, completeness, or usefulness of any information, apparatus, product, or process disclosed, or represents that its use would not infringe privately owned rights. Reference herein to any specific commercial product, process, or service by trade name, trademark, manufacturer, or otherwise, does not necessarily constitute or imply its endorsement, recommendation, or favoring by the DOE or Battelle Memorial Institute. Trademarks belong to their various owners, and are not specifically identified herein. The DOE encourages wide dissemination of the technical information contained herein, with due respect for Publisher's rights regarding the complete work.

PACIFIC NORTHWEST NATIONAL LABORATORY
Operated by
BATTELLE MEMORIAL INSTITUTE for the
UNITED STATES DEPARTMENT OF ENERGY
Under contract DE-AC06-76RLO 1830

Library of Congress Cataloging-in-Publication Data
Human choice and climate change / edited by Steve Rayner and Elizabeth L. Malone.
    p. cm.
  Includes bibliographical references and index.
  Contents: v. 1. The societal framework – v. 2. Resources and
technology – v. 3. The tools for policy analysis – v. 4. What have
we learned?
    ISBN 1-57477-045-4 (hc: alk. paper). ISBN 1-57477-040-3
(softcover: alk. paper)
       1. Climatic changes—Social aspects. 2. Human ecology.
  3. Environmental policy. I. Rayner, Steve, 1953–. II. Malone,
Elizabeth L., 1947–
  QC981.8.C5H83   1998
  363.738'74—dc21   97-49711
                                                   CIP

	Hardover	Softcover
Four Volume Set	1-57477-045-4	1-57477-040-3
Volume 1: The Societal Framework	1-57477-049-7	1-57477-044-6
Volume 2: Resources and Technology	1-57477-046-2	1-57477-041-1
Volume 3: The Tools for Policy Analysis	1-57477-047-0	1-57477-042-X
Volume 4: What Have We Learned?	1-57477-048-9	1-57477-043-8

Printed in the United States of America.

Battelle Press
505 King Avenue
Columbus, Ohio 43201-2693
614-424-6393 or 1-800-451-3543
FAX: 614-424-3819
E-Mail: press@battelle.org
Home page: www.battelle.org/bookstore

These volumes are dedicated to Chester L. Cooper and to the memory of William R. Wiley, mentors and friends whose vision and support made this work possible.

Contents

Foreword

The International Advisory Board

In contrast to other state-of-the-art reviews of climate change research, this project sees the world through a social science lens. This focus is reflected not only in the subject matter, but also in the authors' approach. It is a fundamental assumption of the project that the social sciences have ways of defining and analyzing the issues grouped under the term *global climate change* that are distinct from, yet potentially complementary to, those used in the natural sciences, and that social science analyses can generate findings of relevance to the policy-making community. The unique contributions that a social science story of global climate change can make include the awareness of human agency and value-based assumptions; a willingness to grapple with uncertainty, indeterminacy, and complexity; the consideration of social limits to growth; and the distinctiveness of an interdisciplinary social science approach.

We have been involved with this project from its early stages and have met to consider various aspects of the product on several occasions. The importance of social science research in formulating policies that are realistic and implementable can hardly be overstated. Thus, we have insisted that *Human choice and climate change* be policy-relevant. We hope that it will stimulate new scientific approaches to the processes involved in reaching and adhering to environmental agreements. Climate change impacts will be felt regionally and locally, and responses to these changes will be effected at these levels as well. Therefore, widespread understanding of the issues and potential choices is extremely important; focusing on the social dimension is critical for understanding them.

A social science framing of global climate change will help to make both natural and social science more relevant and more effective contributors to the policymaking process. Reflexive interdisciplinary research that recognizes the rich array of human motivations, actions, and perspectives can supply information that will better support the challenges of decisionmaking under sustained conditions of indeterminacy such as those surrounding global climate change.

FOREWORD

We are pleased to have been associated with this project and hope its products promote the same level of thoughtful consideration that they did during our meetings and discussions of these challenging and significant issues.

The International Advisory Board

Dr Francisco Barnes
The Honorable Richard Benedick
Professor Harvey Brooks
Dr Jiro Kondo
Professor the Lord Desai
  of St Clement Danes
Professor George Golitsyn

Pragya Dipak Gyawali
The Honorable Thomas Hughes
Dr Hoesung Lee
Professor Tom Malone
The Honorable Robert McNamara
Professor Richard Odingo
Professor Thomas Schelling

Preface

When the Pacific Northwest National Laboratory (PNNL) established the Global Studies Program in 1989, I initiated an agenda to develop an integrated understanding of the important new linkages between human and natural systems, linkages that are affecting the evolution of both systems. To this end, the program encompassed the full range of the climate issue, focusing particularly on a sensible coupling between an understanding of the climate system itself and the human decisions that might affect it. This led a decision to assess the state of the art of the social sciences, in terms of their contribution to research on, and understanding of, the climate change issue. Thus, in the winter of 1993, as part of the Global Studies Program effort, the program launched the enterprise that, in due course, became *Human choice and climate change.*

This effort focused on what the social sciences have contributed to the climate change debate and on their potential to contribute more. My hope was that, at a minimum, the work would contribute to the development of a social science research agenda based on more than a call for funding parity with the physical sciences. I was also concerned that the finished document be directed not only to the academic community but also to the policy community.

From the very outset, the object was not to seek the creation of a consensus document of the kind developed by the Intergovernmental Panel on Climate Change, but rather the individual points of view on the climate issue from our 120 authors and contributors, representing a score of countries. Through their direct participation and from a host of peer reviewers, we now have a snapshot of the social sciences in the mid-1990s commenting not only on climate change but also on many aspects of sustainable development.

It is clear from these volumes that economics is by no means the only social science discipline that has relevant things to say about the issue of climate change. Despite the academic language and perspective, the pages of this document have put a human face on the climate change issue.

Some of the authors address social science itself as an issue, rather than social science contributions to climate change research. Indeed, a superficial reading of this material might cause some to question the credibility of social science in addressing climate change issues. For example, rather than speaking directly to the question of human behavior and climate change, the social sciences seem to have a penchant for placing climate change within a larger context, to consider climate change together with many other issues on the social agenda.

Human choice and climate change also reveals the social sciences to be a heterogeneous set of research programs, in which climate change research varies from being a peripheral issue to a highly refined subdiscipline with strong interdisciplinary connections to the natural sciences.

While the physical and natural sciences have been pursuing the questions of how much humans might affect climate, how fast these changes might take place and what the regional effects of these changes might be, our authors have added another question: even if we knew how climate were to change, what could we do about it and how would we decide to do it? Our assessment is that this question, among others, reveals a lack of fundamental knowledge of how society operates, and merits addition to the climate change research agenda.

The enterprise has borne fruit in ways that could not have been foreseen. It addressed the state of the art of the social sciences with regard to the climate change issue, but it also brought together social scientists in the pursuit of a collective goal; it has spotlighted strengths and weaknesses in social science research programs dealing with climate change; and it has laid the foundation for a substantive program of future climate change research.

The editors have conscientiously attempted to reflect the views of the many authors without endorsement or censure. PNNL is pleased to have provided a forum for the expression of a wide range of views and diverse, sometimes even contradictory, conclusions. We thank the International Advisory Board for its wise guidance. The editors, authors, contributors, and peer reviewers deserve substantial credit for striving to bridge and link fields of inquiry that have grown up in isolated traditions.

Gerald M. Stokes
Associate Director
Pacific Northwest National Laboratory

CHAPTER 1

Why study human choice and climate change?

Steve Rayner & Elizabeth L. Malone

Why the concern with climate change?

Time and again over the course of the past decade, climate change has been described by scientists, environmentalists, and politicians as a threat unprecedented in human experience. Tolba's (1991: 3) statement is representative of such concerns: "We all know that the world faces a threat potentially more catastrophic than any other threat in human history: climate change and global warming." Many reasons and combinations of reasons are advanced for this claim, especially the potential rapidity of temperature rise, the irreversibility of change once the forces are set in motion, the geographical scale of the threat, the complexity and nonlinearity of the natural systems involved, the ubiquity and strength of human commitment to combustion technologies, and the political challenges of global cooperation that climate change seems to demand. The real danger, say many, lies in the potential for catastrophic surprise.

Similarly, several candidate causes have been identified. Emissions of greenhouse-related gases from human activities constitute the proximate cause, of course. In the background lurk possible underlying causes: population growth, overconsumption, humans' inability to control the technologies they have created, their inability to implement environmentally benign technologies, their unwillingness to spend current wealth to benefit future generations, their powerlessness to forge effective international agreements and abide by them. Whatever the cause, climate change is framed as a problem, which admits the possibility of solution.

Solutions come in many forms and approach the problem from different angles. Solutions to scientific problems take the form of improved knowledge, understanding, and predictability of natural systems. Solutions to technological problems require innovation and commitment of resources. Solutions to problems of societal cooperation and coordination are offered in the form of international treaties and policy instruments such as taxes or emissions controls. However, all solutions imply choices that must be made, consciously or unconsciously, enthusiastically or reluctantly, and with levels of information that may be satisfactory or unsatisfactory to the choosers.

Why the concern with human choice?

The possibility of human choice, albeit constrained, underlies all of these discussions; that is, humans can choose to respond to the prospect of climate change and can decide, with undetermined and perhaps undeterminable degrees of freedom, what steps to take. However, choice does not merely underlie any possible solution to climate change; it also underlies the problem itself. Increasing global greenhouse gas concentrations are the result of myriad choices that compose the history and contemporary operation of industrial society. Any attempt to change the course upon which human society appears to be embarked requires not only new choices about future actions, but also understanding of past choices—the existing social commitments that have set the world on its present course. The possibility, indeed the inevitability, of choice lies at the core of the climate change issue.

Everyone makes choices about accepting participation in any sort of society (even rebelling against it). Much of human life is devoted to negotiating within families, laboratories, firms, communities, nations, and other institutions the particular balance of independence and interdependence that each person is willing to accept. This tension, characteristic of all forms of social existence, is thrown into stark relief by the controversies that rage and the choices that must be made about the potential for climate change. Questions of choice, therefore, lie at the heart of not only the climate change issue but also the social sciences.

Possible choices with reference to climate change can be grouped into three broad categories, which can be combined in various ways:

- Do nothing. Some say that concern about climate change is unwarranted; the science is unproven, based on speculation bolstered by models so inaccurate they cannot reproduce historical shifts in climate. Others believe that impacts will be gradual, easily accommodated through technology, or insignificant on a global scale. If climate change does occur, then piecemeal adaptation will suffice. Even some who do believe that climate change is likely and may be disruptive suggest that the aggregate benefits of allowing climate change to run its course would outweigh the costs.

- Mitigate, that is, lessen emissions to reduce the magnitude of climate change. If one is convinced that anthropogenic emissions are giving rise to climate change, the obvious direct solution to the problem is to reduce net emissions. Motivations for preferring this option include not only its directness but also, perhaps more importantly, that it can be conjoined with favored solutions to other perceived problems, such as population growth or the income disparities between industrialized and less industrialized nations.

- Anticipate and adapt; that is, change crops and growing regions, retreat from or defend coastal areas, prepare for population shifts and health impacts. Advocates of anticipatory adaptation also regard it as an opportunity to develop policies and technologies that would be beneficial in any event, such as infrastructure that is more resilient to extreme weather events.

For all three strategies, or any combination of them, it makes sense to invest

3

in new knowledge. Improving the accuracy of climate forecasting may confirm that humans need not take any concerted action. Mitigation may require developing new technologies that will allow economic development while reducing the anthropogenic contributions to climate change. Society could invest in geoengineering techniques or large-scale removal of carbon dioxide from the atmosphere. Anticipatory adaptation will require foresight about impacts and new technological and social developments to respond to them.

But who should choose among the possible responses and combinations of responses to climate change? Since it is a global issue, the obvious decision-makers are the governments of nation states who have enjoyed legitimacy as the arbiters of high policy throughout the modern era. People habitually turn to their governments to choose goals (such as emissions reductions) and policy instruments (e.g., a carbon tax). Often climate change research among the social sciences focuses on the macro level of national and international political choice. Certainly the knowledge of how choice processes and mechanisms operate at these levels is valuable in framing issues and conducting negotiations.

However, research at the macro level may reduce important dimensions of social choice to simple instrumental issues. For example, the fundamental concept of fairness, as the glue holding societies together, may be reduced to an instrumental factor affecting the efficient implementation of the goal of emissions reduction. Furthermore, who chooses when the nation state or the market fails to produce a solution? The slogan, "Think globally—act locally" expresses the widespread recognition that choices are made at the micro level, by individuals and groups in particular places. Even in the context of national or international regulations, firms, families, communities, and citizens choose how to respond to incentives and sanctions. Moreover, other institutions, such as environmental organizations, can choose to respond in more robust ways and to try persuasive strategies so others will act voluntarily to comply with or even exceed statutory requirements.

Behind all such questions about choices associated with climate change lurk general questions about how societies and institutions choose the choosers and confer legitimacy upon their decisions. These are problems of collective choice. Choices are embedded and intertwined in social institutions of all kinds, including interest groups, pressure groups, lobbies, elected officials, citizens, and so on. Choices are often so deeply entrenched in societal norms that people will resist persuasion and coercion aimed at changing their behavior.

In part, the role of the social sciences is to probe these background choices by providing the capability to continually examine and re-examine our assumptions, that is, to provide what social scientists call "reflexivity" about societal choice. In the case of climate change, the social sciences remind us to question assumptions and propositions that those who are already committed to a course

4

of action may take for granted. For instance, the conscious choice of responses arises only after we have chosen which issues to take seriously. How do people choose from among a large set of possible problems to work on as scientists, activists, entrepreneurs, homemakers, or politicians? How do individual choices influence what happens at a societal level? What roles do cultural and institutional processes play? How did the choice set of possible or potential issues come to be framed? How did other issues get to be excluded or incorporated into others? With regard specifically to climate change, various questions about choice are intertwined, for example:

- How do scientists choose to study climate change? How do they form a scientific consensus?
- How do people decide that climate change is worthy of attention?
- How do people attribute blame for climate change and choose solutions?
- How do people choose whom to believe about climate change and at what level of risk do they or should they choose to act?
- How do people and institutions mobilize support for (or against) policy action on climate change?
- What is the relationship between resource management choices and climate change?
- How do governments establish where climate change stands in relation to other political priorities?
- How are climate change policy instruments chosen?
- Why and how did the international community choose to address climate change?
- How do societies select technologies that cause, mitigate, or assist adaptation to climate change?
- How can research on social or collective action be useful to the global climate change debate?

Understandably, those who are unshakably convinced, either that climate change is an urgent and impending catastrophe or that talk of climate change is merely, to quote one US Congressman, "liberal claptrap," are likely to be impatient with such questions. For almost everyone else concerned about the issue, such questions may be the starting point from which society can work to make wise decisions about its future.

Different disciplines approach the kinds of questions that we pose from different perspectives, frequently simply modifying or fine-tuning the tools already in hand to account for choice. Issues of human needs and wants, the social bases for cultural or institutional choices, uncertainty, imperfect knowledge, and irrationality are often elided because they are too difficult to represent in equations and computer models.

As we venture among the social sciences, we run into rival prescriptions about how such choices ought to be made (e.g., by experts, by majority vote, by consensus, by preferences revealed in the marketplace) as well as the criteria to be used (e.g., the greatest happiness of the greatest number, or safeguarding individual or majority rights). In this sense, the social sciences reflect the diversity and the unity of human societies, institutions, and individuals on the issues of human choice facing the prospect of climate change.

The problem of collective choice has usually been framed as one of aggregation or of coercion:

- how to aggregate individual preferences into a collective preference, or
- how to persuade individuals to conform with normative requirements of corporations and governments, as implemented by the decisionmakers who are their officials.

Arrow (1951) has famously demonstrated the impossibility of aggregating individual preferences into a collective one in a way that satisfies certain minimal conditions of rationality and transitivity. For Arrow, the dictatorial social welfare function is the only one possible. However, dictatorship is incompatible with democracy. We seem to be caught in a bind. But Arrow's analysis assumes that preferences are inherently individual. If we use another set of assumptions—for example, that preferences are inherently relational (that is, expressions of social solidarity)—we change the nature of the problem from being one of aggregating individuals to discerning the structure and dynamics of social solidarity, which in turn may open up a new solution space for the problem of collective action.

Social science has long been confronted with the central issues of choice and constraint, and, thus, climate change is far from being a unique problem for the social sciences. Moreover, the individual–society tension within the social sciences often reflects a theoretical and methodological gap between the mindsets and methods of various social science disciplines. Even within disciplines, social science paradigms differ in their views of collective action. The problem of understanding and choosing a course of action with respect to climate change is that of articulating choices and consequences across the local and global levels.

For some analysts, social choice is an issue of aggregating individual preferences (from citizens to nations), whereas for others it is rather a problem of decomposing national or communal preferences into appropriate units of social solidarity, such as the household, the village, or the firm. It is pointless to ask which approach is right and which is wrong. Like wave and particle explanations of light, each offers insights that the other cannot reproduce. The characteristics of light's wave and particle properties cannot be simultaneously measured, yet both sets of properties are essential to understanding the behavior of light. Similarly, it is important to understand the sources and consequences of the divergent social science approaches to explaining human behavior so that climate change researchers and practitioners can capitalize on the strengths of that diversity.

The conceptual architecture of this assessment

Human choice and climate change is a climate-oriented assessment firmly rooted in the social sciences. That is, it takes as its starting point human social conditions around the world. Instead of examining the physical and chemical processes of climate change, this assessment looks at climate change in the broader context of global social change. Analysis of climate change needs to be conducted in the context of mainstream social science concerns with human choice and global (not just environmental) change. A global developmental and environmental perspective can be helpful to policymakers and scholars for at least two reasons:

- Social systems intersect and interact with several natural systems simultaneously and interdependently. Human activity therefore represents a crosscutting system constituting major linkages among natural cycles and systems. Hence, changes in human activity stimulated by interaction with one such system tend to influence others in potentially significant ways.
- The scale and rate of change in social systems may well outpace the scale and rate of climate change for the foreseeable future. For example, even vulnerable populations and vulnerable natural resources may plausibly be more directly affected by general economic conditions than by climate change over the course of the next hundred years.

The entry point of a global social science perspective allows us to set our bounds very widely. For instance, in the social sciences, the topic of "climate change" encompasses people's perceptions and behavior based on the threat (or, in a few cases, the promise) of such change, as well as the causes, processes, and prospective impacts of the change itself. In *Human choice and climate change*, we broaden our scope beyond that of the Intergovernmental Panel on Climate Change (IPCC) Working Group on the Economic and Social Dimensions of Climate Change (Bruce et al. 1996) to include research that, although relevant, is not focused specifically on climate change itself. At the same time, we have retained the orientation of climate change as an important policy issue that can act as a touchstone or reference point for theories and research.

Just as the same physical object confronted from different angles may present very different appearances to an observer, so can the same problem be very differently defined when viewed from different paradigms. One strategy for our assessment would have been to accept the conventional framing of the human dimensions of climate change in terms of proximate causes and impacts. Most extant texts concerned with the human dimensions of climate change or, more broadly, of global environmental change begin with a summary of the way that the natural sciences describe the changes that are occurring on the land and in the atmosphere and oceans (e.g., Jacobsen & Price 1991, Stern et al. 1992). These assessments draw directly on the natural sciences to frame the issues for social science inquiry. However, the authors and contributors to this project opted for a riskier approach of attempting to define climate change and, by extension, global environmental change from a thoroughgoing social science perspective.

We seek to learn from approaching the natural sciences from a social science viewpoint rather than through what has been the more orthodox approach of wading into the social science waters from the conventional terra firma of the natural sciences. In so doing, we do not seek to subvert the findings of the natural sciences or discover some social pretext to dismiss societal concern about climate. Rather, we seek to provide an additional footing from which the intellectual landscape of the climate change issue can be viewed. We have tried to complement the natural science perspective, not to replace it with another single vantage point.

Human choice and climate change is presented in four volumes. In the first three volumes, our goal is twofold: to create a text that could serve as an overview of social science relevant to global climate change for researchers with backgrounds in the natural sciences or in the social sciences but not as those backgrounds relate to global climate change; and to provide a reference work for both scholars and practitioners as they perform research, conduct negotiations, or plan and implement policies. To accomplish this goal, the assessment seeks to:

- Represent the range of social science research applicable to global climate change
- Provide insights into the world as viewed through the lens of social science topics, tools, and data
- Review what is currently known, uncertain, and unknown within the social sciences in relation to global climate change
- Assemble and summarize findings from the international research communities of industrialized, less industrialized, and newly democratic nations
- Report these findings within diverse interdisciplinary frameworks
- Relate research results to policy issues and problems.

The fourth volume provides an editorial overview of the first three, reflexively focusing on the challenges that climate change issues present to the intellectual organization of social science, the lessons that the social sciences can bring to understanding climate change issues, and the implications of all of this for policymakers.

In each volume, we have sought to present the subject at a level of detail and theoretical sophistication to make the assessment useful as a reference work for scholars. We have also attempted to tie the material to practical issues useful to decisionmakers and their advisors. We are acutely aware that in aiming the assessment at two audiences we run the risk of pleasing neither. To the first audience we may seem simplistic, even instrumental in our approach. We may strike the second audience as excessively abstract and academic. However, it is our hope that the dual focus of this assessment can be fruitful in pointing to convergence between scholarship and action.

Human choice and climate change, volume 1: the societal framework

Volume 1 of *Human choice and climate change* begins our inquiry into social science perspectives and climate change with an assessment of the state of the Earth's social, cultural, political, and economic systems, which provide the context that supports and consists of the activities that contribute to the emissions of greenhouse gases and within which:

- climate change is perceived and debated
- the impacts of change will be experienced
- human beings will make the critical choices about their future, including choices about how to confront the prospect of changing climate in a changing world.

Climate change is occurring in a complex and rapidly changing framework of human choices that shapes people's perception of it and the opportunities for human response. The social context of climate change and knowledge about it are usually taken for granted. Subjecting it to social science analysis reveals the extent to which our understanding of the science, diagnoses of underlying causes, and views of appropriate action are not merely technical judgments, but embody deep-seated social commitments that provide the context for response options.

"Science and decisionmaking," the first chapter, examines the social processes by which technical knowledge about climate change (and other science-based issues) is created by scientists and communicated to policymakers. The authors begin with four interlocking questions that remained unasked, even unacknowledged, in earlier assessments of social science and climate change:

- How do scientists and their societies identify and delimit distinct problems related to climate change that are considered amenable to scientific resolution?

9

- How do scientists come to know particular facts and causal relationships regarding climate change and to persuade others that their knowledge is credible?
- How do conflicts over risk arise, and how are responses to them handled in a world of conflicting and plural political interests?
- How do human societies and their designated policy actors draw upon scientific knowledge to justify collective action on a worldwide scale?

The authors describe the role that the production and dissemination of scientific knowledge have played in the elevation of climate change to a topic of worldwide interest and political concern. Their analysis reveals how the normal model of the relationship between science and policy, which has been termed "speaking truth to power," assumes that the two domains are and should be largely distinct. However, social science analysis indicates a level of interdependence between science and politics so strong as to constitute a process of co-production of relevant knowledge, which most often occurs unrecognized by either scientists or policymakers.

Science and technology studies demonstrate how scientists build on local experiments and knowledges in laboratories and field studies to formulate generally accepted methods, facts, and theories. Through a process of standardization and network building, scientific knowledge can attain a universal validity, as climate change science has through the deliberations of the IPCC. Applying insights from studies of the social processes of scientific inquiry, the chapter examines the implicit assumptions embedded in theories and models used to study interactions between the biogeophysical and social systems. Making these assumptions explicit provides an opportunity to question them and to examine their validity in the specific situations to which the theories and models are being applied. This reflexivity is important because scientific research that fails to engage in such self-examination risks becoming irrelevant to the world beyond the laboratory or academy walls. Perhaps worse, it leaves science susceptible to political backlash against scientific consensus on climate change—just as has happened in the US Congress. Policymakers who rely on data from unreflexive research risk errors in their decisionmaking that may cost them (and the societies in whose name they act) dearly, whether financially, politically, or socially.

 The interdependence between scientists and policy-makers constitutes a process of co-production of knowledge seldom recognized by either.

"Population and health" and "Human needs and wants," the next two chapters, demonstrate that neither of the standard diagnoses of the underlying causes of climate change—overpopulation and overconsumption—can be justified by social science research. Chapter 2, "Population and health," lays out the world's changing sociodemographic profile, the social science controversies about the role of population in climate and other environmental change, and the micro-scale factors that shape peoples' preferences about family size and spacing of children. Although the authors find that rapid population growth has a negative effect on the development of many, albeit not all, less industrialized countries, the extent of this effect is difficult to quantify, or even to demonstrate on a global scale because of the complexity and multiplicity of relationships involved and the variability of local circumstances. The authors conclude that population policy has too often been based on the easy, specious logic "You would be happier if you had fewer children," which cannot be justified by rigorous social science evidence. The real underlying logic is often "I would be happier if you had fewer children."

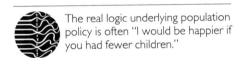

The real logic underlying population policy is often "I would be happier if you had fewer children."

Population, as such, is not the issue shaping climate change or other environmental degradation. The appropriate question is how are population factors mediated through institutional and social structures to affect natural resources and the environment? In some areas population makes a big difference to environmental impacts; in others it does not. Where it does make a difference, the costs and benefits of intervening directly to affect population must be weighed against the costs and benefits of policies designed to loosen institutional rigidities that prevent families from responding flexibly to the pressures of population growth. The people most vulnerable to impacts of climate change tend to be members of impoverished populations living in environmentally fragile zones of less industrialized countries. These populations already adapt very flexibly to the impacts of extreme climatic fluctuations, such as storms and droughts, albeit at considerable cost of human life and suffering. But climate change may overstretch their coping capacity. Although it is quite unlikely to change the big picture of world population size, rate of growth, and age structure, climate change will have an impact on mortality, fertility, and migration at regional and local levels.

If the impact of population is less than straightforward, what can be said about consumption? What justification is there for distinguishing consumption for survival from luxury consumption? Chapter 3, "Human needs and wants," evaluates the attempts of various disciplines to establish human needs as the basis for climate policies compatible with individual fulfillment and societal development. The authors show that the concept of basic human needs has universal rhetorical appeal, but it cannot made operational coherently in a way that helps policymakers to define climate policy goals. Everyone may agree that clean air, access to potable water, a minimum ration of calories and protein—even entitlements to atmospheric carbon sinks—are all somehow basic human needs, but in practice it is impossible to devise universally standardized measures for their operationalization. How clean is clean? How pure is potable? What constitutes access? What is the age and level of activity of the individual to be fed?

Only by understanding the essentially social character of needs, wants, and their satisfaction through consumption can analysts and policymakers lay the basis for behavioral change.

Furthermore, needs and wants cannot be usefully distinguished. Needs turn out to be wants that someone is unwilling to give up. So long as social scientists and policymakers continue to treat wants as private appetites, they cannot understand how wants come to be standardized in society and how those standards change. The issue of how societal preferences change is a critical one for long-term modeling and for policy interventions that seek to alter either the scale of consumer demands (including demands for small or large families) or the technologies by which demands are satisfied. If consumption choices are recast—not as private preferences but as public statements establishing or confirming community identity, group membership, or social solidarity—then fundamental changes in consumption patterns are likely to require very basic changes in the kinds of society people live in. Only by understanding the essentially social character of needs, wants, and their satisfaction through consumption can analysts and policymakers lay the basis for behavioral change.

The authors of Chapter 3 focus attention on the emergence of new models of wealth, based on the notion of social capital, that includes the levels of social support that people can expect from the communities and institutions to which they belong (rather than focusing on dollars per individual). Criteria for measuring social capital are being explored; however, they have not yet reached the level of development or received the recognition already being given to the valuation of natural capital and so-called green accounting.

. . . debate about climate change is often a surrogate for a broader, so-far intractable political discourse about population, lifestyles, and international development.

The broader "Cultural discourses" about climate are the subject of the fourth chapter, which probes deeper into societal controversy over diagnoses and prescriptions and exposes the social commitments that underlie the range of opinions and political positions. In the course of debating climate change at home, at work, in the media, or in the halls of power, experts and lay people alike diagnose the underlying human causes of climate change as lying in population growth, profligate consumption, or incorrect pricing and property rights allocations. In response to these diagnoses, participants in these cultural discourses seek prescriptions to remedy climate change while protecting competing principles for procedural fairness as well as distributional and intergenerational equity. Disagreements about the underlying human causes of climate change and proposed solutions to it are deeply rooted in competing institutional narratives about nature as well as rival principles of fairness. The chapter illustrates that debate about climate change is often a surrogate for a broader, so-far intractable political discourse about population, lifestyles, and international development.

In elucidating the various voices of experts and lay people in the climate change debate, the chapter demonstrates that the basis for such discourses is essentially institutional. The authors make a strong claim that social relationships, rather than individual preferences, stabilize the public expression of values about what is natural and what is right. How people bind themselves to each other simultaneously shapes the way they bind themselves to nature. Social and cultural variables of network density, interconnectedness, and rule sharing account more effectively for variations in environmental perceptions and behavior than do standard demographic variables such as age and sex. To guide the reader through this novel landscape, the authors present a conceptual map of human values to help social scientists identify and track the strength of support for alternative positions and to help policymakers identify opportunities for effective intervention in the debates.

Public information campaigns that assume that discrepancies between lay and experts accounts of climate change are simply attributable to knowledge deficiencies are bound to fail.

The social science perspective represented in this chapter suggests that public information and education campaigns to change people's energy use or other environmentally relevant behavior fail because changing behavior is not simply a problem of removing exogenous barriers to the natural flow of knowledge. The social science perspective redirects efforts at communication from simply overcoming ignorance to creating shared frames of reference and opportunities for shared action. Public information campaigns that assume that discrepancies between lay and experts accounts of climate change are attributable simply to knowledge deficiencies are bound to fail.

Climate discourses are complex and turbulent. Many voices join in, and they are often inconsistent, even self-contradictory, but not randomly so, nor in a way that can simply be ascribed to naked self-interest. By labeling the present state of affairs as disorderly, each voice seeks to legitimate the reordering of society along its own preferred institutional principles. How these institutional arrangements are structured and operate in the climate change arena is the topic of Chapter 5, "Institutions for political action," which ties the value commitments of climate discourses to the institutional arrangements that human beings use for making collective choices about society and the environment.

The growing prominence of global environmental issues as matters of high politics is itself a sign that the nation state retains an important and powerful position. However, the character and the role of the state are changing rapidly in fundamental aspects of its international and domestic roles. Political influence and real power is diffusing to international and domestic policy networks in which governments and their agencies interact directly with social movements, firms, and communities. The notion of unitary national interest is increasingly difficult to sustain. The rising importance of nonstate actors and the emergence of aspects of a global civil society, in the light of global climate change, are now garnering much attention from sociologists and international relations scholars alike.

 The real business of responding to climate concerns may well be through smaller, often less formal, agreements among states; states and firms; and firms, nongovernmental organizations, and communities.

The new landscape of world politics—and global environmental politics in particular—has given voice to those formerly marginalized or excluded from political dialogue. The authors conclude that, although the Framework Convention on Climate Change represents an important expression of worldwide concern about climate and the persistent issues of global development that are inextricably bound up with it, the real business of responding to climate concerns may well be through smaller, often less formal, agreements among states; states and firms; and firms, nongovernmental organizations, and communities.

However, this response process is likely to be messy and contested—not that messiness or contestation are to be disparaged. Patterns of interest-group mobilization and representation help to sustain a bias in favor of activities that lead to increasing greenhouse gas emissions. The status quo is insulated from fundamental change by the influence of routines, established procedures, and traditional and close ties among economic and political elites. Climate policies as such are bound to be hard to implement. Simply incorporating climate change into existing political agendas is unlikely to produce the desired outcomes. Similarly, presenting climate change measures as ways of achieving higher taxation or welfare expenditure is also likely to meet significant opposition. True win–win solutions prove to be elusive. Effective actions designed to mitigate or respond opportunistically or adaptively to climate change are likely to be those most integrated into general policy strategies for economic and social development.

Volume 1 places climate change in the dynamic context of a changing societal landscape that shapes changes in the atmosphere. Here the responses of political and social institutions are crucial, and human choice must be taken into account. Sometimes the separation of the biogeophysical systems from the social systems has led global climate change researchers to focus on climate change as if it were the most important issue facing the sustainable development of human society. Yet sustained consideration of one issue can be maintained only at the cost of excluding others. Decisionmakers need to consider the opportunity costs as well as the benefits of directing their present attention to climate change. Furthermore, for most of humankind, climate change is not life's most pressing issue, certainly not on a day-to-day basis. A social science framing of the problem introduces a more complex view by asking what else is going on in the development of human society and how climate change will affect and be affected by these societal changes. Volume 2 looks at climate change in relation to human resource use, and opportunities to reduce human impacts on the climate and climate impacts on humans, particularly through a broadly defined conception of technological change.

Human choice and climate change, volume 2: resources and technology

Volume 2 of *Human choice and climate change* anchors both the climate change issue and social science approaches to it in the context of the Earth's resources: climate, land, water, energy sources, and materials used in technologies. Climate change is the result of fundamental human choices about the conversion of energy and human occupation of the Earth's surface. These activities have been identified as both the proximate causes of greenhouse-related emissions and the sites of primary impacts on human activity.

Chapter 1, "The natural science of climate change" summarizes the present state of the international scientific consensus about climate change, drawing on the findings of the Second Assessment Report of the IPCC, as well as on other research. The social processes that go into producing and standardizing this kind of scientific consensus are described in the first chapter of Volume 1. Current scientific claims about climate change and its impacts introduce Volume 2 because it focuses on the major resource systems, or human support systems, that enable people to live as they do on the Earth: that is, land use, occupation of coastal zones, energy production and use, and the processes of technological change. As human systems, these are no less institutional systems than the ones examined in Volume 1. However, each is perhaps more directly dependent on constraints and opportunities presented by natural systems than (with the possible exception of population) the frameworks presented in Volume 1. Thus, it is appropriate at this point to introduce material from the natural sciences that social scientists should be aware of in analyzing and understanding the human dimensions of climate change.

This chapter explains the greenhouse effect, the results of greenhouse gas emissions on radiative forcing, and the mechanisms by which forcing translates into climate change. The complexities of these processes are further compounded by emissions of aerosols, the role of clouds, and interactions of gases in the atmosphere. Furthermore, the natural variability of climate is an undisputed fact, so the possible human contributions must be analyzed in the context of natural changes.

The current scientific consensus is that the global mean surface temperature has increased by 0.3–0.6° Kelvin (K) over the past century. The global temperatures in recent years have been among the warmest in historical records and probably one of the warmest periods in the past six hundred years. However, the warming is not uniform over the globe, with some areas even experiencing a cooling. The understanding of this climatic change is a high priority in the natural science community. Although the signal is still emerging from the noise of natural variability, recent studies suggest that the current changes in climate are indeed related to human activities, including the emissions of carbon dioxide and other radiatively important gases and aerosols.

The chapter goes on to outline the potential effects of changes in various climatic factors, specifically sea level rise, human health, agriculture and food supplies, water resources, and nonagricultural ecosystems. Although knowledge is improving in these areas, many aspects of climate change remain highly uncertain. In particular, the regional changes in climate expected from global climate change are poorly understood, as are the impacts on humanity and the biosphere.

 Although the signal is still emerging from the noise of natural variability, recent studies suggest that the current changes in climate are indeed related to human activities.

The next four chapters trace the origins of climate change in human behavior at aggregated and disaggregated levels and focus on the potential impacts of climate change on fundamental human systems of productivity.

Chapter 2, "Land and water use," examines human activities that increase greenhouse gas emissions from the use of land and water resources. It also assesses the potential impacts of climate change and climate change policies on land and water use for the production of food, energy, fiber, and construction material, as well as for recreation, aesthetic and spiritual satisfaction, and creation of a sense of identity.

The intensification of land and water use has been a global trend during the five centuries of the colonial, industrial, and postindustrial periods. Today, every accessible hectare and waterway are managed (or deliberately not managed) for human ends. The most remote tundra in the Arctic North and the most forbidding reaches of the Sahara Desert are subject to human management decisions of one sort or another.

Land use and water use are important to global climate change in at least three ways. First, land use affects the exchange of carbon dioxide, methane, and other greenhouse-related gases between the Earth and its atmosphere. Second, agriculture, forestry, and other land-based productive activities depend crucially on surface energy and water balance, which are closely linked to climate. Hence, they are more likely than other human activities to be affected by climate change. Third, projected growth in both population and resource-demands presents important challenges to land and water use in coming decades, whether climate changes or not. Discussions of global environmental change have tended to subjugate the issues of sustainable development of land and water resources to the globally systemic changes of ozone depletion and climate change. Analysts seek to identify no-regrets strategies that would enhance sustainability and at the same time help to prevent or adapt to climate change. Many opportunities exist for sequestering carbon or limiting emissions, although they require a searching analysis of their full social and environmental repercussions.

The chapter concludes that climate change is by no means necessarily the most important challenge to the sustainability of land and water resources. The connections between land use and climate change are important, but should not be allowed to set the land-use research agenda. There is room for serious concern about the adequacy of land and water resources to meet current and likely future demands locally and globally, whether climate changes or not. Around the world, increasing misuse of land and water resources already threatens human welfare in the near to medium term. The apparent failure in these regions of management to forestall such threats underlines the need to study land-use and water-use adaptation strategies, regardless of any efforts

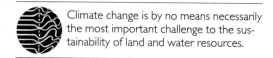

Climate change is by no means necessarily the most important challenge to the sustainability of land and water resources.

toward reducing greenhouse-related emissions. Responses that can address these issues while addressing the challenges of climate change should be a priority for research.

Measures encouraging adaptation to climate change may likewise offer collateral gains in other areas, improved agricultural research being an important case in point, and institutional strengthening to facilitate adaptive shifts in land and water use another. The key lesson of social science analysis is that the constraints on and opportunities for successful response are not only technical, and that influencing land and water use in desired ways requires a sound understanding of how and why these resources are used.

Similar themes emerge from Chapter 3, "Coastal zones and oceans." Coastal regions are particularly important because of high concentrations of human population living close to the sea and their particular vulnerability to potential climate impacts.

Coastal zones have historically generated economic activities that allowed societies to flourish. Many coastal problems now being encountered worldwide result from many people's use of the terrestrial and aquatic resources over a long period of mostly unrestricted development of coastal areas. These problems include the accumulation of contaminants in coastal areas, shoreline erosion, and the rapidly accelerating decline of habitats and natural resources. Population growth and migration associated with economic development places additional demands on coastal areas and resources, posing another threat to the sustainability of these areas. The impacts of unsustainable and often uncoordinated coastal development are likely ultimately to result in the degradation of natural systems that provide protection against the sea, habitat for many species, and food for many people. These impacts could pose significant risks to public health and welfare.

With or without climate change, coastal zones will see further growth in urban areas and increased tourism. The growing population density along the coasts will put further pressure on the resource base, including ocean fishing, wetlands-dependent products, and unique ecosystems and species. This pressure will probably result in deteriorating living conditions for many inhabitants, especially in less industrialized countries. Hence, there are strong imperatives to adopt integrated coastal zone management strategies that will combine responses to growing demands on coastal and ocean resources and the threat of climate change. Local knowledge will be essential to the success of these strategies. The adaptive coping abilities of coastal, often rural, and often nonliterate people have enabled their survival under stress. They have detailed knowledge of local conditions and past responses, as well as the complex and varied patterns of ownership and use of marine and coastal resources. In the policy hierarchy they seldom get their due recognition. Consultative and participatory approaches that include local stakeholders offer challenges and opportunities for both analysis and decisionmaking.

The adaptive coping abilities of coastal, often rural, and often nonliterate people have enabled their survival under stress. In the policy hierarchy they seldom get their due recognition.

The fourth chapter in Volume 2, "Energy and industry," examines global and regional patterns of greenhouse-related emissions arising from the production of goods and services. Over the twentieth century, energy use has become the most important human-generated source of greenhouse gases, especially carbon dioxide produced by fossil-fueled energy generation. Most analyses predict steady increases in worldwide energy consumption over the next several decades. Thus, any attempt to limit greenhouse gas concentrations in the atmosphere must focus on energy supply and demand and the costs associated with reducing greenhouse-related emissions from fossil fuel combustion. There is considerable uncertainty about what the levels of energy use and associated carbon dioxide emissions will be over the next century. Worldwide emissions of carbon from fossil fuel combustion are currently about 6 billion tonnes per year. In the absence of new policy initiatives, emissions projections range from a modest decrease to an increase by a factor of 15 over the next century.

Three complementary methods have been used to forecast the evolution of these changes:

- a top-down economic approach, relating aggregate energy use to fuel prices, labor and capital prices, and various measures of economic activity
- a bottom-up approach, employing engineering calculations on a technology-by-technology basis
- a social-psychological approach, focusing on how and why decisions regarding energy use are made at a more micro level than the top-down approach and embodying a more human-behavioral approach than the bottom-up approach.

In the absence of new policy initiatives, emissions projections range from a modest decrease to an increase by a factor of 15 over the next century.

A decade ago top-down and bottom-up approaches produced dramatically different projections. Since then it has become evident that each approach has its strengths and weaknesses, and various hybrid approaches have been proposed. Assumptions regarding the characteristics and likely rate of penetration of new technologies have been developed, and researchers have started sorting through the various explanations for slower than expected adoption of new technologies. There is still some debate about whether some of these explanations describe market failures or simply reflect indirect costs not typically included in the engineering estimates of using a new technology, but that debate has shifted from one about the analytic method to one about the fundamental assumptions employed.

All analyses point towards a much greater rate of growth in greenhouse gas emissions in the less industrialized countries than in the highly industrialized countries for at least three reasons:

- much higher rates of population growth
- higher rates of economic growth driven by technology transfer from the industrialized countries
- a propensity to pursue development through very rapid increases in the output of the heavy industries required to construct the facilities and infrastructure required to modernize economies.

Despite the greater importance of the presently less industrialized countries in shaping the greenhouse-related gas emissions and concentrations of the next century, analysis of these countries has been seriously undertaken only recently.

Two major research directions would greatly improve the usefulness of the analysis to policymakers:

- more intensive study of the less industrialized countries, where most of the growth in emissions is expected to occur
- improved integration between the economic, engineering, and social-psychological approaches.

The second of these is the topic of Chapter 5.

Whereas Chapter 4 concentrates on modeling energy production and use at the macro level, Chapter 5, "Energy and social systems," scrutinizes energy-related institutional decisionmaking about production and consumption at the level of the firm and household behavior. The chapter highlights the meaning and evolution of energy-consuming practice in everyday life. The authors advocate moving beyond conventional policy-oriented research, focused on the beliefs and behaviors of individual end users, to a focus on people as social actors operating within households, offices, government departments, or other institutions. Such a shift entails viewing energy-related decisions as processes of social negotiation rather than as the result of personal attitudes or enthusi-

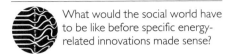

What would the social world have to be like before specific energy-related innovations made sense?

asms. Rather than focusing on energy in isolation, or on the services that energy provides, energy-related practices are instead addressed as forms of consumption, much like any other.

Instead of taking the social goals and purposes of energy consumption for granted, the approaches explored in this chapter call those ends into question. The rationalistic notion that technologies are neutral problem-solving devices gives way to the view that problem and solution are, as it were, joined at the hip. The authors challenge researchers and policymakers to rethink the relationship between policy and energy demand and the way in which energy analysts and policymakers conceptualize the future. Instead of trying to predict the future, the authors advocate efforts to specify the sociotechnical preconditions for a range of possible futures. Rather than seeking to model people's impact on future energy demand, the question would be, what would the social world have to be like before specific energy-related innovations made sense?

Much of the research reviewed in this chapter emphasizes the extent to which the future is already inscribed in existing practices, infrastructures, and cultural arrangements that limit the scope for doing things differently. Together these suggest that, even in the most favorable of circumstances, policy levers that focus on end-users are unlikely to modify the web of interests and histories that surround their choices and habits. But conventional tools and forms of policy analysis configure the conceptual landscape and the perception of possible courses of action, just as the tools and technologies of energy consumption configure their users. Discussion of the human dimensions of energy and global environmental change is currently embedded in a policy paradigm that contains within it a somewhat limited and restricting theory of social and technological change.

The dynamics of technological change have important implications for the expectation of many researchers and policymakers that such change will be important to resolving the issues of climate change. The final chapter in Volume 2, "Technological change," brings these issues into the foreground, illustrating how individuals, institutions, and societies select and reject technological opportunities. The chapter focuses on the important issues surrounding the dynamics of technical change and their outcomes, particularly in relation to attempts to orient technological developments.

"Technological change" begins with the fundamental question, "What is technology?" The answer is that the social sciences conceptualize technology in different ways, ranging from concrete artifacts and skills to more abstract, less nuts-and-bolts notions of technology as material culture or as sociotechnical landscapes.

Artifacts are black boxes that work; they are black boxes because users cannot see beyond their functions to their inner workings or their energy sources. Technological regimes, such as the hydrocarbon-based energy regime, consist of many commitments, sunk investments, and institutionalized practices that evolve in their own terms and are hard to change. Sociotechnical landscapes are the patterns of physical infrastructures, artifacts, institutions, values, and consumption patterns—the material culture of our societies—and the backdrop against which specific technological changes are played out. It is important to include all three levels of understanding technology, because its implication in climate change is as much through sociotechnical landscapes and technological regimes as through particular artifacts such as steam generators or internal combustion engines.

Thus, the conventional technology policy model of technology describes artifacts emerging from research and development establishments and subsequently transferred to the marketplace. However, this model tells only part of the story of technology in society. Other aspects include the processes and conditions of novelty creation, the messiness of implementation and introduction, and the aggregation of myriads of little decisions that underlie the development and embedding of technology in society. All of these elements are part of successful technological transformations that involve growing irreversibility and interdependence among social, economic, and material components of the sociotechnical landscape and that make it very difficult (but not impossible) to consciously direct technological change to meet climate policy ends.

There is no simple technical fix.

In exposing the societal embeddedness of technical systems and highlighting the opportunities and constraints for changing the ways in which humans use energy and the Earth's surface, the final chapter of this volume drives home the fact that there is no simple technical fix. What tools do we have? This question is the topic of the chapters assembled in Volume 3.

Human choice and climate change, volume 3: the tools for policy analysis

Public policy and private decisionmakers often look to the simplifying frameworks of formal tools of analysis to guide their decisions. The third volume of *Human choice and climate change* evaluates the adequacy of the conventional tools of policy analysis for supporting or making prudent human choices in the face of climate change.

Chapter 1, "Economic analysis," describes the strengths and limitations of the most widely applied toolkit of contemporary industrialized society and a substantial contributor to the current state of understanding climate change. "Economic analysis" seeks to explain how the wants of a population interact with the technical means for their satisfaction to produce demand for goods and services; what the scale of that demand, expressed as economic growth, implies for the global environment; and what constraints on growth might result from climate change policies. Proposed policies may be evaluated from a variety of perspectives; a mainstream approach usually includes growth-oriented economic analyses of the costs and benefits. Costs of mitigation in the near and medium term are weighed against often diffuse and uncertain benefits in the very long term, and must account for countries whose economic development may depend upon emissions-generating activities and who may thus be unwilling to trade off growth for emissions reductions. The result of most studies employing cost–benefit analysis is that relatively modest near-term actions are required, although the degree of intervention grows over time.

Global climate change is part of a class of problems that tend to exacerbate the shortcomings of the mainstream approaches to economics,

Other issues for economic analysis include valuing nonmarket (environmental) goods and nonmonetary transactions and assets; global efficiency, trade, and the implications of inequities in the global distribution of income; handling surprises; and the choice of time-cost discount rates, which must be based on social criteria that lie outside of the framework of economic analysis. Global climate change is part of a class of problems that tend to exacerbate the shortcomings of the mainstream approaches to economics, although economic analysis remains a powerful tool to evaluate candidate policy options.

Policymakers have readily adopted the economics approach to analyze future prospects for growth in greenhouse-related emissions and the consequences of attempts at intervention. This useful, if somewhat narrow, focus has been criticized from within and without the economics paradigm for ignoring shortcomings in the assumptions and methodology of economic growth, as well as the insights available from other fields of social science. Confronted with environmental degradation and resource exhaustion, growth practitioners have added depreciation of these resources to the depreciation of capital stock depicted in their models, thus reducing sustainability to a constraint in the opti-mizing problem of maximizing per capita income. Other practitioners have devised means of valuation for nonmarket effects and nonuse values. These values can be included in the conventional calculus of cost–benefit analysis, where they lose their visibility and are often discounted if they grow too large for comfort.

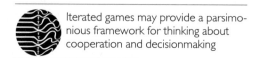

Iterated games may provide a parsimo-nious framework for thinking about cooperation and decisionmaking

Even in its expanded forms, the economic paradigm is essentially based on the concept of the rational individual decisionmaker—the rational actor paradigm. Chapter 2, "Games and simulations," describes frameworks for explicitly exploring the interactions among multiple decisionmakers, in this case nation states, each acting out of self-interest. The authors argue that, although one-shot games are recognized as having very limited application to continuing relations among states, iterated games may provide a parsimonious framework for thinking about cooperation and decisionmaking in situations that fall between the levels of a single benevolent dictator and an anonymous market populated by many well-behaved individuals.

Game theoretic approaches preserve the idea of uniform or universal ration-ality. Often they do not take account of tensions among rival viewpoints and values within a state that can cause it to change course during negotiations in ways that cannot be predicted. Where two-level games have been developed (nesting intrastate games within interstate games), internal differences within states are still framed using the same assumptions about the universality of indi-vidual rationality. Simulations, involving human actors representing diverse experiences as well as interests within teams of players representing national actors, are one way of confronting this limitation. Simulation games, particu-larly when formal models are used within the simulation, can support focused communication among analysts and decisionmakers. Although significant risks accompany these benefits, principally bias and overgeneralization from small samples, simulation-gaming methods have potential value as devices for policy assessment, as supplements to conventional forms of analysis or sober critical reflection.

Both game-theoretic and simulation-gaming approaches move beyond atomistic rationality, but continue to rely on two core assumptions:

- Parties rationally perceive and act on self-interest.
- All of the participants share the same standards of rationality.

Generations of researchers have elaborated this universalistic notion of individual rationality to high levels of sophistication. One of its most prominent features is the rigid separation of reason and values. Chapter 3, "Decision analysis" explores the implications of this separation for global climate policy-making.

The separation of reason and values is deeply entrenched, not only in social science research but actually in the fabric of contemporary culture. Indeed, it has been suggested that the pervasiveness of behavioral sciences based on individualistic rationality derives from their role as *folk sciences*, providing security and guidance to their clientele, largely independent of their effectiveness in practice.

Beginning with the problem of climate risks from the viewpoint of a single decisionmaker who is able to control global greenhouse-related emissions, the authors of this chapter delve into the problems of multiple actors and multiple rationalities. The chapter surveys various social science approaches to the perception, communication, and management of technological and environmental risks, and assesses the potential role of risk assessments and decision rules in formulating climate change policy. In place of individual rationality, many of these approaches emphasize an analytic framework of social rationality in which collective or societal preferences are not merely aggregated from pre-existing individual preferences, but are collectively formulated in daily life and stabilized by institutional arrangements of social solidarity, rather than by the atomized choices of individual human agents.

 Embedding the expertise of risk professionals in a broader social discourse requires appropriate forms of public participation

The authors argue that the basic problem of risk management, global and local, could be tackled in the emerging field of integrated assessment. For this purpose, advanced tools for integrated assessment need to combine the knowledge of experts, decisionmakers, stakeholders, and citizens. Such tools would reintegrate the faculty of reason with the intuition and emotional intelligence rooted in life experience and craft skills. Taking advantage of a broader range of human experiences in the integrated assessment of global climate change requires a critical appraisal of the historical process by which the rational actor paradigm has established an exclusive professional claim for objective knowledge in risk management. Embedding the expertise of risk professionals in a broader social discourse requires appropriate forms of public participation.

Predicting the degree of climate change, even quite accurately, is inadequate for deciding how important its consequences will be for human societies and what, if anything, should be done about it.

This would profoundly move the role of science in society toward what is variously described as vernacular, civic, or postnormal science.

New forms of scientific collaboration engaging universal specialists (scientists) with local specialists (citizens) will require more than a broader decision-making framework. Such collaboration will also require more inclusive ideas of evidence and information. For example, Volume 1, Chapter 1 describes how climate change scientists tend to base much of their argument on mathematical modeling. On the other hand, citizens and politicians tend to draw more heavily on a holistic approach of reasoning by analogy (see for example, Gore 1992). This set of decisionmaking tools is explored in Chapter 4, "Reasoning by analogy." Past experience is a natural, inevitable source of human management strategies. All decisionmakers tend to compare present situations with past experience and adopt similar strategies for seemingly similar situations. Drawing on information about the past relationships between climate and society, researchers attempt to construct guidelines about possible future states, impacts, and coping strategies. The authors find that past climate and society interactions repay the attention of those seeking to understand the human dimensions of global climate change. Historically, the impact of climate as a hazard and a resource has been directly dependent on the adaptive capability of the society affected. It follows that predicting the degree of climate change, even quite accurately, is inadequate for deciding how important its consequences will be for human societies and what, if anything, should be done about it. It also suggests that changes in the characteristics of societies over time will alter the consequences of climate changes, and researchers should be very cautious about projecting potential long-term climate impacts onto the world as it is known today.

These useful insights notwithstanding, significant methodological difficulties arise in drawing rigorous analogies from past human experience of adaptation to climate. Although it is an enormously suggestive resource, the holistic philosophy of reasoning by analogy, almost by definition, makes it very difficult to draw valid comparisons across cases. Valid comparisons of future scenarios require greater formality than is provided by the analogue approach alone. Such formality turns inquiry back in the direction of simplifying models, although not necessarily so simple as the economic models discussed in the first chapter of the volume.

The final chapter of Volume 3, "Integrated assessment," examines the current state of the various modeling tools that contribute to our understanding

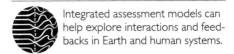

Integrated assessment models can help explore interactions and feedbacks in Earth and human systems.

of the human dimensions of climate change and the operation of climate change policies. Integrated assessment is an issue-oriented approach to research that knits together diverse knowledge from many disciplines to focus holistically on climate change processes. Integrated assessment includes model-based systems, simulation gaming, scenario analysis, and qualitative studies. At present, the dominant integrated assessment activity is computer-based modeling, which draws on multiple disciplines to focus on climate change processes. In that sense, integrated assessment models attempt to emulate the holism of analogies within the more formalized frameworks of (predominantly economic) modeling. Integrated assessment models can help explore interactions and feedbacks in Earth and human systems, function as flexible and rapid simulation tools, foster insights (sometimes counterintuitive) that would not be available from a single disciplinary approach, and provide tools for mutual learning and communication among researchers and policymakers.

Integrated assessment has contributed to the climate change debate by exploring impacts of climate change, mitigation and abatement strategies, issues in cooperative implementation, the likely equity effects of candidate policies, and complicating factors such as aerosols. Models have also provided information on balancing the carbon budget and on various integrated aspects of land use.

However, existing models leave considerable room for improvement. In particular, more satisfactory and representative models of social dynamics and ecological systems, as well as improved treatments of uncertainty, are needed before integrated assessment models can be made more realistic. There is also a need to focus on the factors that shape policymakers' decisions and to include policymakers and other stakeholders in the design and exercise of the models as advocated in Chapter 3.

As scientists develop modeling tools that are more open and flexible, policymakers will be able to use the model results and other insights from different integrated assessment approaches to inform decisions that bear on global climate change and on the social context in which climate change issues are to be considered.

A broad-based approach to integrated assessment embedded in a pluralistic and participatory decision process promises to be the best available guide to policymaking

As a whole, Volume 3 describes the existing toolkit of rational analysis and planning techniques available to scientific researchers and political elites. In so doing, the volume reveals a series of important shortcomings of the toolkit in the face of large complex problems facing multiple stakeholders over intergenerational timeframes. Under such conditions, the mainstream social science tools are presently incapable of providing a reliable basis for rational goal setting and policy implementation. They are overly dependent on a narrow concept of rationality and an approach to policy as the means for making the real world conform to a rational model. The dominant rational-actor approach is in many respects a normative framework masquerading as an analytic one. Social scientists have yet to develop any clearly superior alternatives, but a broad-based approach to integrated assessment embedded in a pluralistic and participatory decision process promises to be the best available guide to policy-making.

Human choice and climate change, volume 4: what have we learned?

The task of preparing *Human choice and climate change* has confirmed the conviction with which we started out, that a variety of social science theories, tools, and techniques, along with different ways of combining them, are essential to move climate change analysis and decisionmaking onto a robust foundation. In this fourth volume, we move into the realm of editorial commentary. We stress that responsibility for these interpretations belongs with the editors alone, although we are confident that all of our authors and contributors endorse most of our selections and emphases.

Our editorial chapters address three questions:

- How does climate change challenge the ability of social science to produce useful knowledge?
- What does social science have to say about global climate change and the debates that surround it?
- What might decisionmakers do differently in the light of our present knowledge of social science and climate change?

"The challenge of climate change for social science" sets out to explore how the intellectual organization of social science and its location in the larger framework of human intellectual inquiry may be constraining the ability of social scientists to realize the full potential of their contribution to climate change research and policy debate. The reasons may lie in the division of intellectual labor that has dominated Western science since the Enlightenment. In the social sciences, this division of labor has resulted in the emergence of two distinctive approaches to subject matter, research methods, and explanatory frameworks. We label these the descriptive and interpretive approaches. Although each potentially adds essential ingredients to humanity's understanding of climate change and related issues, the descriptive and interpretive practitioners of social science seldom communicate with each other, let alone integrate their insights.

Of the two approaches, the descriptive approach is usually considered to be more appealing to policymakers because of its apparent technical neutrality and its ability to generate a numerical bottom line. For example, quantitative analyses of responsiveness to tax rates or the effectiveness of regulation can, in principle, be directly translated into a set of policy choices about whether to implement a carbon tax or appliance efficiency standards and even at what level taxes or standards should be set. Interpretive social science tends to be less readily embraced by policymakers as lacking this potential to provide practical guidance.

But, in fact, the bottom-line solution provided by descriptive research is seldom adopted by policymakers, who actually use such studies to provide background or understanding to their own interpretations and decisionmaking inclinations. Hence, neither kind of social science has any real practical advantage. They merely provide different insights from different standpoints. Making space for both descriptive and interpretive social science in the process of reforming the relationship between scientific research and policymaking offers many advantages.

In "Social science insights into climate change," we draw on the whole of *Human choice and climate change* to elucidate some significant crosscutting themes in social science research related to global climate change. The research and analysis that underpins these themes is developed in detail in the earlier chapters—sometimes in several chapters, as they cover the same issues from different standpoints.

In the grand scheme of things, climate change is probably not the deciding factor in whether humanity as a whole flourishes or declines. The resilience of human institutions and their ability to monitor and adapt to changing conditions seems to be more important. However, changes in regional patterns of habitability are likely to harm poor populations in environmentally fragile areas. Although aggregated global effects may be negligible, regional effects may be severe, including violent storms, inundation caused by sea level rise, and formerly fertile land becoming unsuitable for agriculture.

Global climate change will be inexorable, but also incremental, and will be set against a social, political, and economic background that is far different from the present. In fact, social and political structures and processes will probably

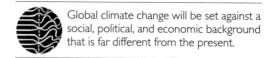

Global climate change will be set against a social, political, and economic background that is far different from the present.

change faster than the IPCC projects for climate. This difference in rates of change may lead policymakers to delay taking action to mitigate or adapt to climate change until disaster overtakes them. However, the same difference also offers the potential to allow societies to stay ahead of climate change, that is, to build in the capability to monitor, anticipate, and respond effectively to changes in many Earth systems resulting from climate change.

Whether or not humanity realizes the potential to get ahead and stay ahead of climate change impacts depends on what happens at the level of decision-making in households, firms, and communities. Diversity, complexity, and uncertainty will frustrate the search for top-down global policymaking and implementation. Social science research in all disciplines indicates that policymakers should attempt to reach agreement on high-level environmental and associated social goals, then look for local and regional opportunities to use policy in various ways appropriate to the institutional arrangements, cultural values, economic and political conditions, and environmental changes.

Overall we find that social scientists have contributed to climate change research by identifying human activities that cause climate change, highlighting environmental changes that affect human welfare, and examining the research process itself and its relationship to policymaking.

Finally, we conclude *Human choice and climate change* with 10 suggestions of ways in which decisionmakers concerned with climate change might modify their goals and approaches to climate policy.

1. View the issue of climate change holistically, not just as the problem of emissions reductions.
2. Recognize that institutional limits to global sustainability are at least as important for climate policymaking as environmental limits.
3. Prepare for the likelihood that social, economic, and technological change will be more rapid and have greater direct impacts on human populations than climate change.
4. Recognize the limits of rational planning.
5. Employ the full range of analytic perspectives and decision aids from the natural and social sciences and the humanities in climate change policymaking.
6. Design policy instruments for real world conditions rather than try to make the world conform to a particular policy model.
7. Integrate climate change concerns with other, more immediate policies such as employment, defense, economic development, and public health.

8. Take a regional and local approach to climate policymaking and implementation.
9. Direct resources into identifying vulnerability and promoting resilience, especially where the impacts will be largest.
10. Use a pluralistic approach to decisionmaking.

Human choice and climate change thus begins with describing the human landscape of the Earth and centers on the role of human choice in the development of climate change as an issue, the definition of causes and likely effects, and the analysis of possible responses. Along with natural science assessments and other related assessments, this social science assessment brings together a wealth of information—but *Human choice and climate change* is not just a report on the state of the social sciences as they have been applied to climate change. Performing an assessment broadens the research focus and generates new insights by the multifaceted analyses and approaches presented here. Theoretical and practical insights that have grown out of the process of producing this assessment can also enlarge the potential application of social science insights and methods to global change—for social scientists, policymakers, and natural scientists.

References

Arrow, K. 1951. *Social choice and individual values*. New York: John Wiley.

Bruce, J. P., H. Lee, E. F. Haites (eds) 1996. *Economic and social issues of climate change*. Cambridge: Cambridge University Press.

Gore, A. 1992. *Earth in the balance: ecology and the human spirit*. New York: Houghton Mifflin.

Jacobsen, H. & M. Price 1991. *A framework for research on the human dimensions of global environmental change*. Paris: International Social Science Council.

Stern, P. O. Young, D. Druckman 1992. *Global environmental change: understanding the human dimensions*. Washington DC: National Academy Press.

Tolba, M. K. 1991. Opening address. In *Climate change: science, impacts and policy*, J. Jaeger & H. L. Ferguson (eds). Cambridge: Cambridge University Press.

CHAPTER 2

The challenge of climate change to the social sciences

Steve Rayner & Elizabeth L. Malone

The climate change issue has challenged the appropriateness of social science paradigms and tools, and the effectiveness of its disciplinary organization. Some types of social science research have fitted in well with the highly visible and influential research into atmospheric chemistry, and physical and chemical processes affected by human activities. For example, computerized climate and environment models have been joined by energy use and economic models. However, other kinds of social science research have remained at the margins of the political and scholarly debate. Although research results are available on, for example, human needs and land tenure systems, these results have not informed the policy dialogue to any great degree. In this chapter we explore an underlying reason why this situation exists. We begin by revisiting the emergence of climate change in the research agenda of the natural sciences and its gradual opening up to social science collaboration.

Following the stimulus of the International Geophysical Year of 1956, the natural sciences evolved an extensive network of research programs focusing on climate and other global environmental changes. Through these efforts, scientists have developed an extensive knowledge base on topics related to climate change in an astonishingly short time. The insights that the natural sciences have provided into the physical and chemical processes involved in climate change and its impacts are necessary inputs for human decisionmaking in these areas. However, prominent natural scientists participating in these programs (e.g., Malone 1985, Clark 1986, Schneider 1987, di Castri 1989) were conspicuous among the voices arguing that natural science information is not fully sufficient to explain the human activities and institutional responses that shape the pattern and extent of greenhouse gas emissions. Natural science information is even less complete with respect to understanding human responses to real and potential impacts of climate change. To address these topics and to inform human decisionmaking in the context of human-induced changes to the atmosphere, they argued, social science research is essential.

Opportunities for social science collaboration in major international scientific research programs addressing climate change, such as the Intergovernmental Panel on Climate Change (IPCC), have been largely focused on extending the framework already established by the natural sciences. The most basic framework consists of a four-box conceptual model: quantified emissions of greenhouse gases, atmospheric chemistry, climate and sea level, and ecosystems. Within this framework (Fig. 2.1), the social sciences provide highly aggregated data on human activities leading to greenhouse gas emissions. These data can be used to drive natural science models of global atmospheric chemistry and physics. In turn, the natural sciences aim to model climatic impacts on managed and unmanaged ecosystems upon which humans depend. At this point, social scientists are invited to project the outcomes of these changes for large-scale

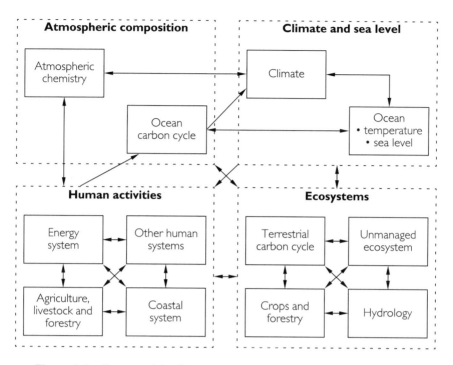

Figure 2.1 Elements of the climate change problem (*source:* Watson et al. 1996).

patterns of agricultural and industrial activity, stimulating macroeconomic and technological responses, which, in turn, may eventually alter anthropogenic emissions estimates. The outputs of such research are presented as data: grist to the decisionmaker's mill. The same framework shapes the bulk of research undertaken within the international social science programs of climate and global change research, such as the Human Dimensions Program of the International Social Science Council (ISSC), which emphasizes stocks, flows, and driving forces of change.

Even though the style of social science emphasized in these programs seems quite compatible with the cyclical framework postulated by the natural sciences, there has been significant concern about the issue of bridging the gap between natural and social sciences, a gap that is invariably taken for granted and associated with much hand wringing. Much is often made of the differences between the two intellectual traditions, exemplified in the distinction between the experimental tradition (including "bench" or laboratory science) and the study of human nature and the history of ideas.

The comparisons inevitably find the social sciences wanting with respect to the characteristics of theoretical consensus about fundamentals, including the nature of phenomena, their measurability and the computability of relationships among them, and the precision and accuracy of prediction. The explanations for these differences range from the charitable observation that social behavior is inherently more complex than the behavior of natural systems to the less charitable assertion that the social sciences are younger and, thus, less mature than natural science.

Since Snow's (1959) classic essay on the "two cultures," we have become accustomed to the idea that the intellectual landscape bequeathed to us by the Enlightenment is bisected by a major fault line between the sciences and the humanities. The exact location of the social sciences in this dichotomy remains, to say the least, ambiguous. For the first half of the century most social scientists aggressively asserted their scientific credentials (e.g., Malinowski 1944, Radcliffe-Brown 1957). More recently, radicals of the right and left have denounced such pretensions. A Conservative British government changed the name of the Social Science Research Council to the Economic and Social Research Council on the basis that, whatever it was that social researchers did, it did not fit Mrs Thatcher's idea of science. At the same time, fashionable postmodernists were pronouncing the impossibility of any comparative social inquiry, let alone any that aspired to scientific basis (see Hannerz 1986).

This chapter argues that, in fact, the social sciences do not fall on one side or the other of Snow's divide, but occupy the uncomfortable space astride it. The conceptual and methodological approaches of modeling the behavior of demographic and macroeconomic systems are essentially indistinguishable from those employed to model changes in the atmosphere or in ecosystems. On this side, social science blends seamlessly with natural science. On the other side, social science concerns with culture and communication ultimately merge into the humanities.

In the climate change debate, this placement of the intellectual rupture between science and the humanities means that some social science research has been used, whereas other research, although relevant and potentially useful, has not been employed in formulating the issues or addressing them. Moreover, the divide, reinforced almost everywhere by disciplinary boundaries, has hampered attempts to formulate a theoretical framework that can be useful to policymakers grappling with the complexities and uncertainties in climate change issues. Because the history and nature of this intellectual divide are directly relevant to social science contributions to climate change research and policymaking, we will briefly review both kinds of social inquiry.

Two styles of social science

The characteristic ways of thinking within the natural sciences and the humanities have diverged over the course of the past three centuries. The internal coherence of both has been enhanced by the insulation of each from the potentially abrasive perspectives of the other. In contrast, the social sciences have led a less comfortable existence, growing up astride the fault, where the tension between knowledge and experience is most acute. Some social scientists have explicitly taken their terminology and ways of conceptualizing from natural science paradigms; others have explored instead the scientific implications of history, philosophy, theology, and other fields within the humanities.

This is not to posit a state of disarray of the social sciences: far from it. The vulnerability of the social sciences is also the source of their strength, in that they do include both kinds of conceptual and methodological approaches. The problem is not the existence of two kinds of approaches, but rather that each has been carefully separated from the other, so that instead of contributing to robust, integrated analyses, scientists who use one approach have tended to stand aloof from researchers using the other approach. Within the climate change debate, the gap between the two styles has meant that relevant research has been bypassed and that researchers dismiss the research of one style or the other on grounds that have little or nothing to do with climate change issues.

Hence, the social sciences are themselves characterized by the uneasy coexistence of the two distinctive approaches of the natural sciences and the humanities—the *descriptive* paradigm and the *interpretive* paradigm. We use descriptive paradigm to refer to research that analyzes social systems in terms of natural science metaphors, e.g. in terms of mass balances, thermodynamics, or stocks and flows. In contrast, the interpretive approach refers to the analysis of the values, meaning, and motivation of human agents.

We can illustrate the difference between the two paradigms by looking at a seemingly straightforward climate change issue—energy from biomass (Table 2.1). A descriptive analysis would investigate the amount of heat energy available from various plants (e.g., short, woody trees or switchgrass), the likely production (tonnes per hectare), the land available to grow such crops, and the price at which biomass becomes competitive with other fuels. An interpretive analysis would investigate the likely consequences of changing the social role of farmers from food producers to energy suppliers, the willingness of farmers to grow biomass, the acceptability to communities of radical changes in the landscape and the presence of biomass-fueled generators, the occupational health and environmental safety risks inherent in the new technology, and the equity implications of policy options such as price supports.

Table 2.1 The different research foci of the descriptive and interpretive approaches, applied to investigation of biomass-for-energy technologies.

Descriptive approach	Interpretive approach
Productivity/yield	Farmers' willingness to grow biomass crops (not food)
Economic viability	Public tolerance of unsightly plantations
Weed control, other management	Priorities for water use and land use
Amount of fossil fuel combustion displaced	Labor-shift hardships on workers and families
Cost of harvesting	Cultural effects of reduced biodiversity
Investment potential	Preferences for other available technologies
Increased soil erosion	
Loss of biodiversity	
Net reduction in greenhouse gas emissions	

The descriptive approach

The descriptive approach primarily uses inventories and accounting systems for the stocks and flows of people, money, raw materials, commodities, and pollutants; for example, Figure 2.2 depicts human and mosquito systems as natural cycles. The uniquely human characteristics of the human system, the abilities to learn and modify behavior, are not seen as pertinent. The descriptive tradition in social science derives from the empirical philosophy underlying natural science descriptions, specifically Newtonian science. Newtonian science is based on the belief that the mind learns everything from what is evident to the senses. English empiricist philosophers, following Locke (1623–1704), postulated that the human mind is a tabula rasa upon which the external world is accurately reflected (Locke 1690). The radical empiricist Hume (1711–76) claimed that all knowledge derives from sensory experience. It has become almost a cliche to observe that Hume's philosophy is a Newtonian science of man. Newtonian thermodynamic determinism is the background of the descriptive tradition in the social sciences.

This approach developed among scholars concerned with wealth, trade, and population in the century following Newton's (1642–1724) formulation of the laws of mechanics and Harvey's (1578–1657) description of the circulation of the blood. Indeed, Quesnay (1694–1774), the key figure among the *physiocratic* economists of pre-revolutionary France, was also royal physician. He drew explicitly upon Harvey's physiology in describing the economy. His *Tableau économique* (1758), is generally considered to be the first schematic description of an entire economy. The physiocratic models departed from previous thinking about the economy in that they did not invoke human choice, desire, and intention to explain the behavior of the economic system. Instead, attention focused on the characteristic operations of the system (i.e., what can be observed and measured).

A generation later, Ricardo's (1772–1823) model of the economy also "elides human intentions" (Gudeman 1986: 45). His concept of the individual is not explicitly elaborated, but the actors in his model, whether landowners, capitalists or laborers, lack intentionality. Ricardo's view of the human is exemplified by his difference with Malthus (1766–1834) over Say's law, according to which supply creates its own demand. For Malthus, demand is not a mechanistic response to supply, because it is made up of both the power and the will to purchase. Ricardo, foreshadowing the declaration of the apocryphal Madison Avenue advertising executive, "If we make it they'll buy it!" maintained, however, that "the will is very seldom wanting where the power exists" (1814 [1952 VI: 133]). Variable tastes and changing desires were not part of Ricardo's image of the human. People would produce biomass and use it as an energy source if it were an economical way to generate electricity.

Ricardo's model moved even further away from concern with human intentions than those of the physiocrats, by his use of a mathematical schema

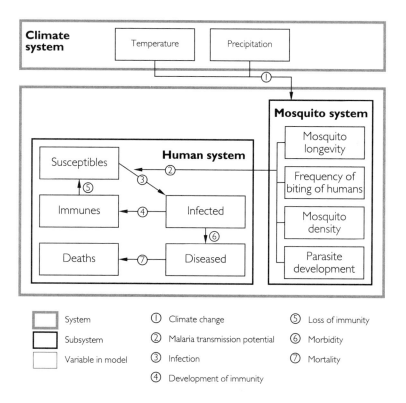

Figure 2.2 A descriptive depiction of climate change health impacts.

that emphasizes form at the expense of content. After Ricardo, economic models took on the mechanical characteristics of closed thermodynamic systems or mass-balance equations.

Following in the steps of the physiocrats and Ricardo, the descriptive approach relies heavily on the ability to count, weigh, and measure things such as numbers of people, tonnes of coal, or barrels of oil. This aspect has led some commentators (e.g., Robinson & Timmerman 1993) to describe the descriptive method as a *physical flows* approach. We do not adopt that terminology here because less tangible elements, such as beliefs and values, can also be represented in the descriptive method as the number of people professing them (e.g. mass survey research or analyses of voting behavior). Knowledge and values reified in this way can therefore be accounted for as stocks and flows.

The descriptive approach has several advantages. The results of descriptive social science investigations are able to draw on the legitimacy of the natural sciences by mirroring the scientific method and the thermodynamic paradigm. Counting and measuring can provide insight into the scope and severity of a problem or locate probable causes among many candidates. Descriptive analysis can compare various pathways from the standpoint of economic efficiency. Its simplifying assumptions and equations can lay out large problems and render them more tractable. And, finally, because description in this sense deals primarily with tangibles, it provides a basis for control; for example, counting tonnes of fossil fuel used can provide a basis for a tax scheme that will limit the number of tonnes burned. This approach is typical of economics and demography and of much of (American) quantitative sociology, descriptive psychology, and quantitative political science. Chapters in *Human choice and climate change* that are predominantly, but not exclusively, descriptive in approach include "Population and health," "The natural science of global climate change," "Land and water use," "Energy and industry," and "Economic analysis."

The descriptive approach in social science and its pre-eminent place in policy analysis arose as part of the larger intellectual effort to devise technologies that could enhance the rational management of nature and society by the emerging modern state. Headrick points out that, "As early as the seventeenth century . . . [governments] encouraged the increase in knowledge of and power over nature" (1990: 59). Headrick listed examples, such as the patent system introduced in England in 1623 and the founding of scientific societies throughout the seventeenth and eighteenth centuries. This was the prelude to a massive increase in the rate of global resource extraction. He continues, "Insofar as technology is knowledge of nature and how to manipulate it for human ends, it follows that countries with the most information are also the most able to develop their economies and transform the land" (1990: 59). The social science

40

technologies of the same period included the new field of statistics, which emerged in the mid-eighteenth century as the practice of inventorying the resources of the state. Merchant (1990: 682) eloquently describes the contribution of the descriptive paradigm to the development of modern political, commercial, and industrial power:

> . . . [W]hen mapped by explorers and cartographers, catalogued and inventoried by militarists and computer scientists, . . . [nature] is controlled by an "eye of power" and subject to unlimited surveillance. Foucault's model of the panopticon of Jeremy Bentham, in which an entire prison can be surveyed from a single central tower, translates to the concept of a cultural overseer.

This stance has been variously described as the separation of the subject from the object, Man/Nature dualism, and instrumentalism. As Latour (1986: 29) observed, ". . . we can work on paper with rulers and numbers, but still manipulate three-dimensional objects 'out there'. . . . Distant or foreign places and times [can] be gathered in one place in a form that allows all the places and times to be presented at once." Thus, the descriptive tradition in both natural and social science separates us from nature and society while providing us with a significant level of control over them. For example, this power is highly concentrated in the computer models that scientists currently use for tracking materials flows and their consequences in both environmental science and macroeconomics (e.g., general circulation models and general computable equilibrium models).

Like all sources of power, this one comes with a price tag—separation of knowledge from the knower. The development of the modern industrial state relied on strategies of control, and modes of mapping, tabulation, recording, classification, and demarcation. These increasing levels of control over nature meant also increasing separation from experiences that should be part of the decisionmaking process. Faced with disembodied parcels of descriptive facts, decisionmakers may become more and more isolated from experience of how myriad decisions transform production and consumption at the level of the community, the firm, and the family. In climate change debates, the hardships of poor people in environmentally marginal areas (deserts, coasts) may be hidden in world GDP statistics. For climate change policies, this has been a source of the disjunction between cost-effective strategies and effective implementation.

Furthermore, the descriptive method is epistemologically realist (Box 2.1). The meaning of belief and value structures and the ways in which they are constituted, reproduced, transformed, and translated into action in social life are

---

Box 2.1 Definitions relevant to descriptive and interpretive social science

Realism: the doctrine that physical objects exist independently of their being perceived and that universals (abstract concepts and the like) exist independently of their being thought about.

Nominalism: the doctrine, opposed to realism, that abstract concepts, general terms, and universals, have no independent existence except as names.

Idealism: the doctrine, opposed to realism, that objects of external perception, in themselves or as perceived, consist of ideas.

---

treated as unproblematic in this approach. Inquiry into these is firmly located outside of the descriptive method within what we refer to as the interpretive method.

The interpretive approach

The *interpretive method* focuses on understanding the meaning that human agents create in the conduct of social life, upon which they build their understanding of their world, and through which they seek to act upon that world. Thus the interpretive method focuses on the nature of experience, the structure of perceptions, the recognition of interests, and the development of frameworks for collective action.

The interpretive tradition in social science emphasizes the essentially social character of the operation of the human mind. The interpretive method is strongest in history, cultural anthropology, and (European) qualitative sociology. In climate change, interpretive analyses have addressed the framing of the problem as well as issues of stakeholder involvement, sociocultural values, the nature and production of knowledge, and policy implementation (research and development investment, technology selection and diffusion, and so on). Chapters in *Human choice and climate change* that are predominantly interpretive in approach include "Science and decisionmaking," "Human needs and wants," "Cultural discourses," "Institutions for political action," "Energy and society," "Technological change," and "Reasoning by analogy."

Because factors such as perceptions, interests, and action frameworks often elude quantification, the interpretive method has often been characterized as *qualitative* social science, contrasted with *quantitative* approaches that we describe as the descriptive method. However, we eschew this particular distinction between the two traditions for three reasons:

- Interpretive social science need not be qualitative (some practitioners having devised sophisticated methods to quantify phenomena that are not as obviously susceptible to counting as heads or barrels are).

- The quantities in descriptive analyses are, in any case, often a numerical representation of a qualitative judgment on the part of the analyst rather than an empirical quantity.
- The distinction between quantitative and qualitative measurement is actually rather fuzzy (e.g., dresses may be sold as small, medium, and large or as sizes 2–16).

The distinctions between descriptive and interpretive approaches can also be rather fuzzy. In fact, within the interpretive approach a researcher can take data of all kinds, quantitative and qualitative, and make coherent meanings that can be used to devise workable arrangements, to effectively address problems, and to set up usable process frameworks. For example, anecdotal and case study evidence can be used to supplement or supplant statistical data. And, of course, the descriptive approach usually includes some interpretive analysis, e.g. in the discussion following the presentation of results and in the conclusions and recommendations of technical reports.

The interpretive tradition derives from philosophical discussions about how human beings acquire knowledge and form (or are formed into) social structures. Although the interpretive tradition can be traced back to classical Greece, the modern interpretive tradition derives from Kant's (1724–1804) disagreement with the English empiricists. Kant specifically rejected Hume's radical empiricist claims that all knowledge derives from sensory experience, insisting instead that reason was itself a capacity of the human mind that shaped experience. Thus, in contrast with the descriptive approach, the interpretive tradition has always distinguished itself by its emphasis on human choice and intentionality. The mind's structuring of sensory experience derives from three sources: the physiology of the human nervous system, the unique historical experience of the individual, and the social and cultural categories and rules that are provided by language and by membership in a family and larger communities.

> Kant introduces a new conception of knowledge. Knowledge does indeed have as a source the Humean element of impressions, the sensory element in which the mind is passive. . . . But Kant continues, there is another element in our knowledge which is derived not from sensory experience. . . . The second element comes from the mind itself. The human mind is not a blank tablet or an empty cupboard as the empiricists Locke and Hume claim. It is equipped with its own pure concepts by means of which it organizes the flux of sensory impressions into substances, qualities, and quantities, and into cause and effects. (Lavine 1984: 193–4)

43

However, although seeking to avoid imposing a deterministic framework on the study of human choice, the interpretive social sciences, exemplified by the philosopher and historian Dilthey (1833–1911), retained their commitment to provide systematic understanding of its manifestations (Selznick 1992: 76):

> Dilthey wanted to uphold the humanist component of historical science without compromising ideals of rigor and objectivity. He thought of interpretation as a disciplined quest for orderly connections in an observable world—a way of doing science, not of escaping science. Yet he often expressed the difference between the human and natural sciences by drawing a sharp distinction between understanding and explanation: "We explain nature, we understand mind".

One of the primary foci of the interpretive method is the understanding of how humans draw meanings out of the data presented to them, emphasizing the sociocultural and institutional (including political) processes involved. The systematic study of such processes yields understanding that can help us make critical choices, knowing what assumptions and decision elements underlie those choices.

As Ryle (1949) suggested, thinking does not take place in the head, but all around us. What we think with is not a private metaphysical mind, but words, pictures, gestures, actions, and both natural and manufactured objects. Indeed we assign symbolic meaning so as to impose some sort of order and coherence on the stream of events. In so doing we sift and filter our sensations of the world. Contemporary studies on the physiology of the mind (Damasio 1994, Edelman 1994) reinforce the physical basis for thinking that can be conjoined with individualistic and sociocultural theories of knowledge and action.

> In the process of making the whole business comprehensible, some perceptions are admitted, some rejected, and others combined or broken down. If we did not filter experiences in this way or make use of public symbols for organizing perceptions and communicating them to others, then we would probably be overwhelmed by the variety of possible interpretations that could be assigned to events. We would have to abandon intellect and discourse and thereby be forced, like the lower animals, to rely on instinct. Mankind would be reduced, as Geertz (1973) has observed, to "mental basket cases" (Gross & Rayner 1985: 3–4).

Different people, of course, organize and assign meanings to their experiences differently. To some, climate change is an impending disaster, and any price is worth paying to avoid it. To others, climate change does not seem threatening, and humankind can probably control any negative impacts. Although we have the same general brain structures and turn our eyes to the same world, there are variations in what we see. As Kuhn says, research shows "that very different stimuli can produce the same sensations; that the same stimulus can produce very different sensations; and, finally, that the route from stimulus to sensation is in part conditioned by education. Individuals raised in different societies behave on some occasions as though they saw different things" (1970: 193).

The interpretive method insists that no standpoint exists outside of history or of society from which they can be independently observed. All organized knowledge, by definition, depends upon socially construed conventions for its organization. In this sense, the interpretive method is epistemologically nominalist. However, most interpretive social scientists use comparison of interpretations to generalize human behaviors.

Style and scale

The descriptive approach derives much of its strength from simplifying assumptions about complex behaviors. It tends to assume homogeneity (or at least a tendency to homogeneity) of human responses to price signals. It is therefore capable of high levels of aggregation in its analyses.

In contrast, the interpretive approach emphasizes variation in human motivation. It explores complexity, sometimes to the point of resisting simplification on principle, regardless of how useful or appropriate it might seem. Indeed, attempts to simplify within interpretive models are often criticized as stereotyping. The interpretive approach therefore tends to produce highly disaggregated analyses.

As a result of their different approaches to aggregation, the two kinds of social science tend to be comfortable at different extremes of scale. The descriptive approach tends towards large-scale analyses, with the nation state (which "grew up with" the descriptive approach) often accepted unquestioningly as the appropriate level for many descriptive analyses. The descriptive approach may be more suited to initial analysis of problems at the global scale; the stance of the observer, and tendency toward aggregation can facilitate analysis at that level.

The interpretive approach, on the other hand, tends to focus on the local scale of interpersonal discourse. Here, the face-to-face community is often regarded as being the natural, self-evident unit of analysis. It is often difficult to demonstrate the relevance of social science at this scale to global-level research agendas.

However, the following case is often made: "Not only that the human activities that drive and mitigate environmental change vary significantly by region or place, but also that historical or local contextual factors are so influential that understanding must be grounded in the specifics of the case" (Turner et al. 1990b: 18). In the last analysis, the activities that drive anthropogenic greenhouse gas emissions are always local, and whatever impacts of climate change affect human populations will be experienced at the local level.

The issue for the social sciences is not merely the assertion of the importance of local-level analysis. As a result of the polarization of the descriptive and interpretive methods, research areas in the social sciences are shaped like an hourglass (Fig. 2.3). That is, theories, methods, and data are underdeveloped at the middle scales between the individual and the nation state.

Furthermore, correspondence between the macro and micro scales is often treated in a simplistic way. The nation state or the firm is often treated as if it were one large individual, with a unitary intelligence and decisionmaking capacity. Or the resources of real individuals may be represented merely by dividing total resource by the number of people, resulting in the creation of a mere "per capitan."

> The image is of a male person, sometimes a homunculus inside each of us, sometimes a gigantic system incorporating the whole of society or the world. Our pervasive microcosm, to whose outlines all our explanations are drawn to fit, is a quintessential stranger; he has no family or friends, no personal history, his emotions are not like ours, we don't understand his language, still less his purposes (Douglas & Ney 1998: in press).

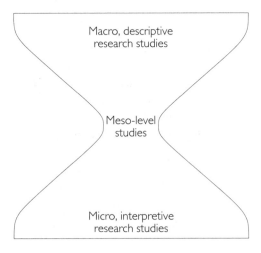

Figure 2.3 Social science research concentrated at macro and micro scales.

For example, in the field of energy modeling, bottom-up analysts project individual behavior onto the national scale (one large individual) whereas top-down analysts assume that the behavior of individuals reflects that of the national population in proportion to their numbers ("per capitan"). Although the names of the modeling approaches seem to indicate macro and micro scales, in fact neither approach is based on a theory of micro–macro scale articulation; both are descriptive approaches that assume undifferentiated individuals.

Local-level analyses, on the other hand, often focus on individuals and small specialized institutions either without regard to their generalizability ("more studies are needed to determine whether similar results can be found in neighboring villages") or their generalizability is taken for granted; that is, village-level solutions are recommended for settings the world over.

Linking the local and the global is often cited as one of the most challenging aspects of climate and other manifestations of global change. Few attempts have been made to validate studies at one end of the scale with those at the other, and sparse are the research studies at the middle levels, especially those that articulate connections among individuals, groups of various sizes and cultural backgrounds, and global-level players in climate change issues. From the perspective of the social sciences, meeting this imperative requires, as a first step, linking the interpretive and the descriptive approaches, using the research approaches and strengths of each, and expanding the reach of study, as appropriate, into various middle scales, with appropriate integration of overlap. However, as discussed in the next section, the viewpoints cannot simply be merged; each makes unique contributions to scientific knowledge.

Style and standpoint

Throughout the social sciences there is poor understanding of the articulation of human behavior at the local level to the behavior of the global social and economic system. Furthermore, available knowledge of local behaviors has not penetrated very deeply into the global descriptive agendas of the IPCC or the Human Dimensions Program of the ISSC.

Linking the local and the global cannot be achieved simply by increasing the scale and quantifiability of interpretive analysis to meet a more thickly textured descriptive analysis as it attempts to accommodate lower levels of aggregation. The gap between the two approaches is not merely spatial but raises fundamental issues of what kinds and sources of knowledge we value as analysts. Contrasting sixteenth-century iconography with contemporary satellite photographs of the Earth, Ingold (1993) illustrates the situation by tracing the change in the standpoint of human inquiry from the Enlightenment to the

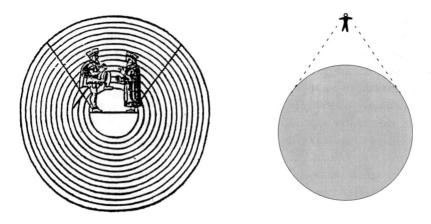

Figure 2.4   Local and global standpoints (*source:* Ingold 1993).

present (Fig. 2.4). In Maffei's *Scala naturale* of 1564, the scholar is shown at the center of the environment consisting of fourteen concentric spheres envisaged to form a giant stairway, the ascent of which, step by step, affords more comprehensive knowledge of the world through experience within it. In modern satellite imagery, the scholar experiencing the world from within is displaced by an observer viewing the world from without.

The problem with this standpoint is that it privileges observation to the exclusion of experience. Local knowledge, originating in experience, is downgraded as partial, parochial, and ultimately unreliable, whereas global knowledge is treated as universal, total, and real. Against this view, Ingold argues that (1993: 40–41):

> The difference between them [local and global perspectives] is not one of hierarchical degree, in scale or comprehensiveness, but one of kind. In other words, the local is not a more limited or narrowly focused apprehension than the global, it is one that rests on an altogether different *mode* of apprehension—one based on an active perceptual engagement with components of the dwelt-in world, in the practical business of life, rather than on the detached, disinterested observation of a world apart.

Returning to the example of biomass energy and its descriptive and interpretive analysts: each analysis assumes that it can predict the feasibility of this novel technology without needing to know what the other knows. The descriptive method aims to determine feasibility through technical modifications and adjustments to the system. The interpretive method suggests that, if people decide to grow biomass and use it to generate electricity, knowledge of the agricultural and industrial systems will be superfluous. Similarly, descriptive analysts will prefer estimating potential energy savings and theoretical technological fixes. Interpretive analysts will call for people to adopt "green" values and change their lifestyles. These different approaches also resonate with political preferences for more analysis before implementing policy and the demand for action now.

But in fact neither approach is sufficient. The technical knowledge of how biomass grows and the energy generation works provides no basis for a change in energy sources; the intentions, commitment, and cooperation of the farmers and utility decisionmakers are as much a part of the equation as are heat potential and roads to the generation plant. Conversely, no matter how much they want biomass energy, people have to be able to grow plants and operate generators. Externalities such as increasing temperatures or changes in precipitation can be described in terms of scope and severity and interpreted as dangerous; but without both description and interpretation, the world will not have energy from biomass.

How can a potential for complementarity be applied to a climate change issue? The descriptive approach provides an absolutely vital link between the social sciences and natural science analyses of climate change. Collaboration between natural science and the descriptive approaches has revealed much about what would happen under various scenarios, but it does not help in choosing among the probable or feasible scenarios. To understand these issues, we also require interpretive approaches that can introduce qualitative and value-related parameters. Both approaches are highly relevant to current negotiations about how to implement the Framework Convention on Climate Change (FCCC).

The FCCC states that "The ultimate objective . . . is to achieve, in accordance with the relevant provisions of the Convention, stabilization of greenhouse gas concentrations in the atmosphere that would prevent dangerous anthropogenic interference with the climate system." Further, "policies and measures to deal with climate change should be cost-effective so as to ensure global benefits at the lowest possible cost." A particular ceiling for greenhouse gas concentrations can be maintained in a variety of ways. Some will be more costly than others. Economic (descriptive) analysis (Box 2.2) can show that it is more expensive for all nations to stabilize emissions individually than for the world to stabilize emissions jointly. But some regions might be better off under an individual stabilization scheme. Descriptive analysis can identify conditions under which populous countries would have an incentive to drop out of an international agreement to control fossil fuel carbon emissions in the post-2000 period, even if emissions rights were allocated on an equal per capita basis. Descriptive analysis can also highlight the need to construct dynamic international

Box 2.2 A descriptive approach to emissions reduction

Economists have begun to examine the problem of optimal policy responses to various possible ceilings on the atmospheric concentration of CO_2. Several important findings are beginning to emerge:
- It is less expensive by half to hold atmospheric *concentrations* below 500ppmv than it is to stabilize *emissions* at 1990 levels.
- Stabilizing emissions at 1990 levels leads to concentrations in excess of 500ppmv after the year 2100.
- An atmospheric concentration ceiling of 500ppmv is consistent with a pattern of emissions that initially exceed 1990 levels.

In the third case, emissions diverge very little from the business-as-usual trajectory until sometime after the year 2010. Before that time, investments in the development of cost-effective low-emission technologies would have to be made so that emissions could be reduced rapidly during the next century and could eventually be stabilized at a level significantly below 1990 emissions.

To keep concentrations below 400ppmv, reductions in global fossil-fuel carbon emissions would have to begin immediately. And for atmospheric concentration ceilings higher than 500ppmv, there is more time to develop technologies, less urgency in radically reducing emissions, and a higher level of long-term emissions.

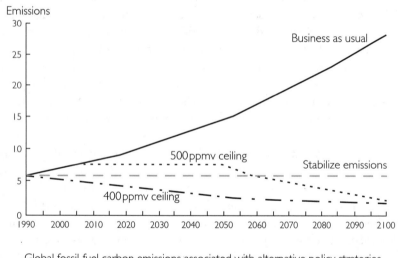

Global fossil-fuel carbon emissions associated with alternative policy strategies.

agreement, capable of being modified as global changes occur and societies evolve. But the descriptive approach cannot successfully explore social and ethical dimensions of different political options and has difficulty dealing with tradeoffs between equity and efficiency.

Similarly, a descriptive analysis of the cost of maintaining the atmospheric concentration of carbon dioxide below various ceilings shows that both the costs and the appropriate and efficient policy response depend on the level that is determined to be "dangerous." However, the analysis cannot determine what is "dangerous," nor can it tell us what might actually be acceptable and implementable strategies to lessen the dangers.

Defining "dangerous" and formulating implementable strategies are highly complex and context-specific processes that defy straightforward quantification and benefit–cost classifications. When evaluating issues such as species loss, habitat degradation, declines in human health, and loss of human lives, benefit–cost analysis proves insufficient. Additional tools are needed that can deal with societal values and with processes and institutional issues, and that can help to analyze why such issues such as the value of human life seem to be intractable.

Redressing the disconnection in style, scale, and standpoint within the social sciences will at least require bringing together the descriptive and interpretive methods. Using and broadening established mechanisms, researchers can adopt either a multidisciplinary or an interdisciplinary approach. In the former, scientists from various fields work together on a problem that has been defined within the framework of one particular discipline. A truly interdisciplinary approach involves people from different fields working on a problem that they have defined together in a way that it cannot be defined from within any single discipline. Interdisciplinary research often yields insights otherwise not attainable.

Perhaps the strongest reason for exploiting the complementarity between the two approaches is the nature of the climate change issue. The dimensions of climate change simply cannot be adequately addressed without using both approaches. *Human choice and climate change* explores descriptive and interpretive approaches and their application to science, human values, and policy discourse.

Social science methods applied to climate change issues

Social science tools, theories, and data draw on both the descriptive and interpretive traditions. There are, of course, no neat boundaries separating the two styles of science, but differences in the conduct of research studies may dispose scientists working within one paradigm to discount the results of research conducted in another paradigm. A challenge to social scientists is to generate research results from both paradigms that are useful to policymakers. Perhaps an even greater challenge is to develop frameworks for decisionmaking that assess both kinds of research to make truly informed choices.

Topics

The choice of topics frames what can be said. A general social science viewpoint opens a range of perspectives; both the viewpoint and the issue itself are then valid topics for discussion. For example, both descriptive and interpretive approaches to information and behavior are valid viewpoints from which to discuss social processes of knowledge creation and use in science policy and everyday life. Topics that deal with population can include descriptive fertility data and interpretive inquiry into the social meaning of having children. Consumption topics can include descriptions of the range of goods people buy and interpretations of the social relations that form the basis for acquiring goods.

The full range of descriptive and interpretive social science includes much research relevant to climate change, but which is generated in other contexts. Social scientists explicitly focusing on climate change usually approach the issue primarily as a substantive topic or as a research site for pursuing inquiries along existing lines. Researchers may frame and orient the research questions to societal arrangements rather than climate change itself. Thus, interpretive social scientists are continually asking whether climate change is really the important locus of research, whether we have formulated research inquiries to yield useful analysis (or, as Gertrude Stein is alleged to have said on her deathbed, "Never mind the answer: what's the question?"), and how science and policy questions are related to each other. Other researchers often respond by questioning whether research that in fact does not focus on climate change is relevant to climate change issues. Some chapter reviewers of *Human choice and climate change* complained, "Climate change is barely mentioned until halfway through the chapter!" Perhaps policymakers expect that social science research will focus more immediately on climate change than natural science assessments that devote extensive attention to basic processes, such as photosynthesis, which may seem quite removed from climate itself.

Tools

The tools employed also affect research results; the choice of tools makes some insights possible but limits other possibilities. Laboratory experiments, for example, can tell us a great deal about specific, controlled situations; however, they may not tell us much about what happens in ordinary human societies. Again, the situation in the natural sciences provides a parallel; for example, the effects of carbon dioxide fertilization under controlled conditions may tell researchers very little about its effects on open-air agricultural crops.

Social science tools encompass a range of approaches, from computer models to surveys, case studies, analogs, games, scenarios, and verbal and visual models or frameworks. All of these tools have been applied to global climate change issues. The most important approaches are exemplified by economic cost–benefit analysis, risk analysis, analogs, games, and integrated assessment (Box 2.3). Examples of more specialized or less well-known tools are briefly described in Box 2.4. In general, the most well-established tools are also those subject to the most detailed criticisms; their weaknesses and their strengths are well known. Tools that have not yet been submitted to the scrutiny of intense use, or to the tendency to expand their use into areas they were not developed for, are often criticized only in theoretical terms.

Data

The social sciences employ a wide range of data, including precise values for such items as income, demographic characteristics, and agricultural yields—but also including values that cannot be measured or can be measured only comparatively, such as human wants, priorities, and comfort. Social facts include information about communication, institutional structure, traditional practices and relationships, and processes of social adjustment. Preference orderings as well as numerical indicators can be social data.

That said, *Human choice and climate change* includes descriptive number sets that describe aspects of people's social and institutional lives. Global-level data have helped scientists and policymakers to look at the scope of the whole climate change issue and to indicate areas where further research and analysis are particularly needed. Although all are rich in information, the numerical data-heavy chapters are "Population and health," "Land and water use," "Coastal zones and oceans," "Energy and industry," and "Economic analysis." For example, demographic data are the starting point for depicting qualitatively different scenarios for the future (see Table 2.1). Data on land use and water use reveal uncertainties and inconsistencies in how people think about natural resource use and they expose needs for developing common definitions and methods in classifying and evaluating various uses. Comprehensive energy data allow researchers to devise multiple strategies for reducing emissions or developing new technologies. And economic data are the basis for calculating costs of alternative policies.

Box 2.3   Mainstream social science tools for climate change research

Cost–benefit analysis provides useful and powerful insights in evaluating for least-cost strategies, but it provides no basis for choosing strategies to be evaluated. Issues within the economic paradigm include measurement of informal markets, (in)equality in global distribution of income, nonmarket valuation of environmental goods, consumer sovereignty, accounting for sociocultural factors, and ecological impact considerations. The discount rate makes a huge difference in cost–benefit analysis over climate change timescales, but economics has no method for determining what is the right discount rate to use in any particular case.

Economic analysis of markets in the sense of neoclassical economics provides a powerful means to understanding the economic behavior of large numbers of unconstrained actors with access to good information about supply, quality, and price. But additional nonmarket tools also help to explain the nonmonetary meanings and values assigned to goods of various kinds for which prices, especially those related to land use and water use. Although economists have attempted to account for environmental goods by assessing people's willingness to pay or to accept compensation for such goods, the accounting methods are not well established. Indeed, setting monetary values on environmental goods at all may be unacceptable to many people.

Energy models are well developed for studying the behavior of energy systems. An energy–economic model treats energy like other economic goods, whereas an energy–engineering model focuses on technologies of energy production and consumption. Both kinds of models are essentially descriptive. However, reconciling global analyses and country studies is currently beyond the state of the art. Endogenous technological change can significantly affect estimated mitigation costs.

Simulation-gaming methods can serve as supplements or alternatives to formal modeling in assessing such uncertainties. Simulation games, particularly when formal models are used within the simulation, can also support focused communication between analysts and decisionmakers; general improvement of this communication may hold substantial value of a diffuse and long-term nature. But significant risks accompany these benefits, principally bias and overgeneralization from small samples.

The *rational actor paradigm* is the only widely used framework for the study of economic phenomena and the most influential framework for the study of many other phenomena. However, it provides less insight into the relationships among risks, costs and benefits, and risk bearers than other social science tools of risk management, such as psychometric analysis, cultural theory, arena theory, and social amplification theory, which look at the synergies within the portfolios of risk that are carried by individuals or institutions.

Analogues can lead to insights into how societies deal successfully or unsuccessfully with climate change, but analogues must be chosen with care. Presently no unambiguously useful analogues to global scale climate change exist, although they are often evoked in the debate in attempts to demonstrate a line of reasoning or a particular point.

Integrated assessment, comprising multiple strategies, is a powerful tool for analyzing and evaluating different emissions and mitigation paths, including cost efficiencies; for investigating the outcomes and costs of international cooperation in carbon control and emissions mitigation; and for handling complexities such as the cooling effect of sulfur emissions.

Box 2.4   Examples of emerging social science tools for climate change analysis

The vicious circle model ("Population and health") describes a situation where low status of women implies high fertility, high fertility implies poverty, and poverty reinforces the low status of women. A virtuous cycle model is also possible, where changes in agricultural production stimulate new technologies and increase prosperity, resulting in improved status of women, higher education, and other social advances.

Understanding people as "intentional systems" ("Human needs and wants") allows us to account for social interactions, the embeddedness of social systems in each other, their layers and many dimensions. Analysis of policy options can then evaluate more of the complexities and uncertainties, reducing the risk of perverse or unintended outcomes.

The sociotechnical landscape matrix ("Technological change") visually accounts for social needs, knowledge, skills, and infrastructure essential to our concept of technology, allowing more productive intervention to encourage effective technological responses to global change issues.

Social-psychological energy analysis ("Energy and industry" and "Energy and society") focuses on explaining past and future trends in energy service demands within a framework that includes the full range of human activities, comprising both individual and social influences. This approach sheds light on why consumers change their preferences; its downside is its large data requirements.

Industrial ecology ("Energy and industry") is a concept in which interactions between human activities and the environment are systematically analyzed. In industry, the approach accounts for all material inputs and outputs, including wastes, seeking to be more efficient and environmentally "friendly" at the same time.

Vulnerability analysis ("Coastal zones and oceans" and "Reasoning by analogy") assesses the potential for negative outcomes or consequences of hazards such as climate change. One focus is on the elements of resilient systems, which have low vulnerability, either resistant to hazard effects or capable of coping with them.

Myths of nature ("Cultural discourses") systematically characterizes cultural views of nature: liable to collapse, robust to shocks, or robust within limits. These categories help explain the polar positions within the climate change debate and can help in framing policy to address multiple points of view.

Map of human values/tripolar policy space ("Institutions for political action") is a visual representation of sets of values that shape both diagnoses of and prescriptions for climate change issues. Such a map can inform and facilitate negotiations by assessing the distance between positions and possibilities for common ground.

Science and technology studies ("Science and decisionmaking") locate and bring out assumptions that may be hidden but are crucial to understanding the issues and limits of research results.

Policy network analysis ("Institutions for political action") attempts to shed light on the relationships among governmental and intergovernmental participants in the policymaking process. These relationships are often informal, strongly institutional, and important in formulating problems and structuring policy responses. The opening and closing of these networks give the policy community its dynamic qualities.

Table 2.2 Social sciences data on population: alternative assumptions for life expectancy at birth in 13 world regions.

	1995	2000			2000–35			2000–85		
		L	C	H	L	C	H	L	C	H
Male										
North Africa	62.7	63.0	63.8	64.7	64.6	71.1	77.7	64.6	74.9	85.2
Sub-Saharan Afr.	50.6	49.6	51.1	52.6	43.1	54.4	65.6	43.1	58.1	73.1
China and CPA	66.4	66.9	67.2	67.4	70.2	72.0	73.9	70.2	75.8	81.4
Pacific Asia	63.1	63.1	64.1	65.1	63.1	70.6	78.1	63.1	74.4	85.6
Pacific OECD	76.1	76.6	77.1	77.6	79.9	83.6	87.4	79.9	87.4	94.9
Central Asia	65.1	65.6	66.1	66.6	68.9	72.6	76.4	68.9	76.4	83.9
Middle East	65.6	65.9	66.7	67.6	67.5	74.0	80.6	67.5	77.8	88.1
South Asia	59.7	59.7	60.5	61.2	59.7	65.3	71.0	59.7	69.1	78.5
Eastern Europe	67.3	67.8	68.3	68.8	71.1	74.8	78.6	71.1	78.6	86.1
European FSU	61.1	61.1	62.1	63.1	61.1	68.6	76.1	61.1	72.4	83.6
Western Europe	72.1	72.6	73.1	73.6	75.9	79.6	83.4	75.9	83.4	90.9
Latin America	66.3	66.8	67.3	67.8	70.1	73.8	77.6	70.1	77.6	85.1
North America	72.3	72.8	73.3	73.8	76.1	79.8	83.6	76.1	83.6	91.1
Female										
North Africa	65.3	65.6	66.4	67.3	67.2	73.7	80.3	67.2	78.7	90.3
Sub-Saharan Afr.	53.9	52.9	54.4	55.9	46.4	57.7	68.9	46.4	62.7	78.9
China and CPA	70.1	70.6	71.1	71.6	73.9	77.6	81.4	73.9	82.6	91.4
Pacific Asia	67.4	67.4	68.4	69.4	67.4	74.9	82.4	67.4	79.9	92.4
Pacific OECD	82.2	82.7	83.2	83.7	86.0	89.7	93.5	86.0	94.7	103.5
Central Asia	72.5	73.0	73.5	74.0	76.3	80.0	83.8	76.3	85.0	93.8
Middle East	68.0	68.3	69.1	70.0	69.9	76.4	83.0	69.9	81.4	93.0
South Asia	59.7	59.7	60.7	61.7	59.7	67.2	74.7	59.7	72.2	84.7
Eastern Europe	75.0	75.5	76.0	76.5	78.8	82.5	86.3	78.8	87.5	96.3
European FSU	72.8	73.3	73.8	74.3	76.6	80.3	84.1	76.6	85.3	94.1
Western Europe	78.6	79.1	79.6	80.1	82.4	86.1	89.9	82.4	91.1	99.9
Latin America	71.5	72.0	72.5	73.0	75.3	79.0	82.8	75.3	84.0	92.8
North America	79.1	79.6	80.1	80.6	82.9	86.6	90.4	82.9	91.6	100.4

Source: Lutz (1996).
L = low, C = central, H = high.

Linking science and human values

Despite the emphasis on methods and data, at the human level climate change is ultimately an ethical issue. Just as technical analyses and arguments prove insufficient to persuade communities to use imported technologies, human decisions about the threat of climate change are never merely technical. They are decisions about equity, what is fair in our relationships with each other and about natural ethics, what is right with respect to our relationships with nature.

Although the analysis and description of ethical systems as social phenomena belong in the social sciences, the normative exercise of ethical reasoning is traditionally the province of philosophy and theology. Thus, bridging the gap between the descriptive and interpretive traditions in social science—and even exploiting the commonalities between interpretive approaches in the social sciences and the humanities—is an imperative for effectively linking the practice of scientific and moral reasoning in confronting global climate change.

A further practical imperative to integrate the descriptive and interpretive methods is the need to understand human choice in social change, as well as aggregating market behavior and mapping demographic change. Following in Ricardo's footsteps, the descriptive method assumes continuity of human preferences and consistency of human behavior over time. The descriptive models do not seek to explain what humans value and therefore cannot anticipate sudden ruptures in social behavior resulting from changes in values and the institutional arrangements that embody those values, or to assess the potential for changing human motivations through political or other forms of social intervention. Because the vast array of human behavior is effectively compressed into drivers and responses, the descriptive approach encourages the adoption of descriptivist kinds of explanations for the actions of social systems and the individuals within them. Hence, policy prescriptions based solely on the descriptive paradigm are limited to instrumental tinkering with technology and prices.

But, as we have emphasized in the previous chapter, social systems involve *human choice*; unlike a billiard ball shot across a table or an electron orbiting the nucleus of an atom, a human being has the ability to make conscious decisions about the directions in which he or she is moving and at what speed. Although social decisionmakers are often constrained by their own paradigms and the initial conditions of the problem they are attempting to resolve, the existence of human choice means that their actions cannot be accounted for in purely deterministic terms.

Values in science

Human choice also raises a methodological problem for the construction and operation of descriptive social science. Science, whether natural or social, is conducted by humans and is thus itself subject to human choice. Humans choose what to study and what to ignore, what methods to use in their analysis and what criteria to apply in determining the validity of the data gathered. For instance, do we study energy conservation or geoengineering? Do we assess quality of life or longevity? Must we have an untreated control population or can we learn from studies that treat all subjects?

In making these choices, researchers and decisionmakers inevitably make value judgments. However, when the value-based assumptions embedded in the theory or model disappear into the background, they come to be seen as "natural" and are uncritically accepted, often without any conscious thought about either their presence or their implications. Indeed, the more scientists reduce human choice to a preference for low prices (e.g., within energy models), the more they are interfering as agents. Since humans cannot stand outside of history and society to observe and describe them, the insights of interpretive social science are essential to make the underpinnings of analysis as explicit as possible.

Interpretive social science brings to the conduct of scientific inquiry an awareness of the impact of human choice, by introducing *reflexivity* into the research and policymaking processes. As defined in Chapter 1, reflexivity is the self-conscious examination of the implicit assumptions that are inevitably embedded in any analytical approach. In the descriptive approach, assumptions may be systematically laid out (population growth, GDP, energy efficiency improvement, and so on), but they are typically unquestioned within the research study. This is consistent with the outside observer stance of the descriptive researcher. However, if these assumptions are made explicit, the researcher has an opportunity to question them, rather than taking them as given. The interpretive contribution of keeping assumptions visible adds meaning to the research results by providing clear boundaries and caveats. Thus, if research in the two paradigms can be integrated, a more complete analysis can be accomplished.

Furthermore, strong linkages between the two can provide a further bridge to rich resources within the humanities that can also help to deal with fundamental issues such as social justice. Research in the humanities is linked with social sciences in the thought of deep ecologists and ecofeminists, for example. Centering on an environmental debate, scholars have used arguments about the right relationship between humans and nonhuman nature, arguments that rely on evidence from theology, moral philosophy, and literary imagery as much as on scientific data. Sociological, political, and image-rich arguments are blended. These kinds of linkages can increase understanding of the moral and ethical underpinnings of scientific knowledge.

The descriptive approach works effectively only when scientists take their assumptions for granted so that they can structure experiments that will have meaning within those assumptions. "Acting scientifically means acting on the assumption of a determinate nature waiting to be described by a neutral observation language" (Fish 1994). In the natural sciences, Kuhn notes "that once the reception of a common paradigm has freed the scientific community from the need constantly to re-examine its first principles, the members of that community can concentrate exclusively upon the subtlest and most esoteric of the phenomena that concern it. Inevitably, that does increase both the effectiveness and the efficiency with which the group as a whole solves new problems" (1970: 163–4).

Humans must reproduce and extend cultural conventions that are unquestioned in everyday life to successfully develop in and adapt to society.

As Alfred Whitehead has said in another connection, "It is a profoundly erroneous truism . . . that we should cultivate the habit of thinking what we are doing. The precise opposite is the case. Civilization advances by extending the number of important operations which we can perform without thinking about them." This is of profound significance. . . . We have developed these practices and institutions by building upon habits and institutions which have proven successful in their own sphere and which in turn become the foundation of the civilization we have built up. (Hayek, quoted in Koford & Miller 1991: 22)

However, although in daily life the ability to do more things with less deliberation may be a sign of technical and social development, it also increases the danger of unwelcome surprise. The interpretive social sciences have the capability to make the implicit explicit, to provide society with the tools of reflexivity and to enhance society's resilience to shocks.

Combining the reflexivity of the interpretive with the instrumental knowledge of the descriptive method seems an obvious course for improving our understanding of the human dimensions of climate change and use in policymaking (Box 2.5). A reflexive social science drawing effectively on both the descriptive and interpretive methods could help identify the multiplicity of characteristics needed to achieve a successful solution and the political problems, both immediate and longer term, associated with varying alternative climate management strategies.

Utility-based and rights-based approaches to decisionmaking

The descriptive and interpretive approaches respectively embody quite different normative imperatives for decisionmakers. The tendency of the descriptive paradigm towards high levels of aggregation gives rise to a top-down decisionmaking rationality. The quantitative aspect of the paradigm leads to an essentially utilitarian perspective on decisionmaking. That is, the practice of inventorying the stocks and flows of goods and bads creates the conditions for a decision framework based on a technique for calculating societal happiness measured by their distribution as introduced by Bentham (1748–1832). The rise of utilitarianism as an explicit decisionmaking principle in the eighteenth and nineteenth centuries paralleled the development of systems of national accounting and statistics. These systems were designed to assess and facilitate the development of industrial capitalism, but they also held out the prospect of civil or corporate leaders being able to rationally assess the impact of decisions on the well-being of the statistical population.

Box 2.5 Two social science approaches—descriptive and interpretive

Social science research in the human dimensions of global change may be of two types.

The descriptive approach starts at the macro level in describing the stocks and flows of population, resources, wealth and information through time and space. This approach is widely recognized as being closely compatible with natural science approaches to global change.

The interpretive approach, beginning at the micro level, focuses on motivations, the creation and interpretation of information, and the development of shared understanding as the basis for human actions that ultimately shape the stocks and flows.

Because the two approaches are so different in kind, there has traditionally been little cross-fertilization between them. Models in both kinds of social science are simplifications in order to further analysis of more complex cases. Simplifications tend to be more accepted in quantitative models; in qualitative models, they may be seen as mere stereotypes. Descriptive models, which tend to be mathematical or quantitative, are incomplete in that they cannot account for the full variety of descriptive variations among diverse human populations. Interpretive models, which tend to be verbal or qualitative, are also incomplete in that they are seldom capable of powerful generalization from their micro-level studies.

We therefore see significant potential progress in understanding to be gained from research that integrates these two approaches.

A short step turned the possibility of such a means for calculating what would contribute to the greatest happiness of the greatest number into the imperative to pursue that goal. The solution that provides the greatest happiness of the greatest number also must be an efficient solution, since any departure from efficiency, also by definition, reduces the amount of good available for distribution. "A bias toward the value of efficiency is inherent in the methods of policy analysis and utilitarianism has been the ideological position most forthrightly incorporating this standard as a central value" (Heineman et al. 1990: 38). However, efficiency is not merely a technical issue or an indication of rational behavior within utilitarianism, but is also an intrinsically moral imperative that arises from the descriptive paradigm itself.

Hence, the development of the descriptive paradigm in social science and public administration created the possibility of utilitarian decisionmaking and provided a moral imperative for its application. During the same period, public policymakers were increasingly coming under the direct scrutiny of electors as public offices increasingly opened up to election by expanding (although by no means universal) franchises. Public policymakers thus became increasingly aware of the direct expression of happiness or discontent within the constituencies that elected them. The utility principle is by definition an aggregative approach, seemingly ideally suited to guide the government of the nation state of the eighteenth and nineteenth centuries and the first half of the twentieth centuries. Similarly, the rapid expansion of the joint stock company increasingly

60

rendered the managers of business enterprises subject to censure of shareholders. Thus, the democratization of civil authority and the need to expand capital resources in industry and commerce both provided practical reinforcement for the utility principle. To put it bluntly, the greatest happiness of the greatest number became the key to retaining elected office.

Thus, the utility principle domesticated moral diversity for decisionmaking authorities by offering the capability to measure and monitor the stocks and flows of societal good, the usual proxy for "good" being wealth in some form. In many climate change analyses, GDP is the accepted aggregate measure of well-being. By the same process, decisionmaker awareness of alternative ethical considerations was systematically attenuated. The imperative to provide for societal good at the highest level of aggregation provides no guidance for securing the happiness of minorities and individuals, even of those individuals in the happy majority. "The guiding criterion for policy is the greatest good for society, quantitatively defined. But contemporary utilitarians, primarily economists and theorists of public choice, like Bentham, still have no principle for distributing this social good according to manifest principles of equity" (Heineman et al. 1990: 40).

In contrast, the tendency of the interpretive tradition to focus on the face-to-face community rather than the nation state directs the attention of scholars working in that paradigm to the particular circumstances of decisionmaking rather than to the aggregate outcome. Attention to disaggregated particulars articulates smoothly with an orientation towards bottom-up, rather than top-down, decisionmaking. In climate change discourse, scientists report stories of individuals, families, and villages—far removed from total or per capita GDP. The insights of the interpretive paradigm are more likely to be of interest to those who espouse libertarian or egalitarian ethics, emphasizing the rights of the individual or the minority in the face of majority preferences, as, for example, in Kantian ethics and the Jeffersonian political tradition in the United States. Hence, the interpretive paradigm is often associated with a critical stance toward the status quo, and is often equated with and labelled as the "critical" tradition in social science, which marginalizes its significance by definition.

Increasing insight into the diversity of motives, values, and preferences of individuals actually tends to frustrate utilitarian social accountancy, which depends on blending out such distinctions in the process of aggregation. "Most utilitarians assume, like the adherents of the politics of interest, that the sole legitimate basis of social good is what individuals happen to value. And they view the process of social choice as an aggregative one, in which individual preferences are added to one another in arriving at decisions on the substance of social welfare" (Heineman et al. 1990: 71). It is hardly surprising therefore, that the insights of the interpretive paradigm are not merely considered

61

irrelevant to, but actually have to be excluded, from utilitarian decisionmaking in order to preserve the rationality and legitimacy of the utility principle.

Hence, the distinction between two social science paradigms is not merely an artifact for the history of ideas or a scholarly distinction of mere academic interest. It actually lies at the heart of the crisis of governance that pervades the local, national, and global communities at the close of the twentieth century, that is, the tension between interdependence and independence, between pursuit of the greatest happiness of the greatest number, and the assertion of individual, local, or ethnic rights that ought not to be violated, even at the expense of the aggregate good. Is it more important to reduce GDP losses or to prevent the displacement of the population of the Maldives? Whereas Kant's principle that every person is to be regarded as an end in him or herself is generally recognized as a form of the doctrine of human rights, Bentham dismissed the concept of rights as "plain nonsense; the imprescriptible rights of man, nonsense on stilts" (Russell 1946: 742). He denounced the articles of the Declaration des droits de l'homme as falling into three classes: " (1) Those that are unintelligible, (2) those that are false, and (3) those that are both."

Similar vituperation for the social inefficiency of rights-based ethics is not unheard of among contemporary utilitarians. For example, in response to proposals by Bullard (a sociologist) that current inequities in the distribution of environmental burdens on minorities and the poor should be addressed on an environmental rights basis, rather than according to risk-based criteria, Nichols, an economist, responded (1994: 267):

> This framework has considerable popular appeal, but *it ultimately is counterproductive from the perspectives of both society as a whole and even the specific groups it tries to champion.* Moreover, it provides little practical guidance to environmental decisionmakers trying to set priorities. . . . Bullard's proposed environmental justice framework makes continued inequities in protection more likely . . .

Bullard replied (1994: 260) that his proposals:

> . . . are no more regressive than the initiatives taken in the nineteenth century in eliminating slavery and "Jim Crow" measures in the United States. This argument was a sound one in the 1860s when the 13th Amendment of the Constitution was passed despite the opposition of proslavery advocates, who posited that the new law would create unemployment (slaves had a zero unemployment rate), drive up wages (slaves worked for free), and inflict undue hardship on the plantation economy (loss of absolute control of privately owned human property).

Clearly these are not merely technical arguments about the best way to clean up the environment. Similar clashes between the utilitarian and rights-based views arise over the projected costs of climate change. In response to damage estimates that climate change will result in a decline of global productivity of less than 1 percent over the course of the next century, utilitarians have expressed the view that only low-cost mitigation measures can be justified. On the other hand, those who espouse a rights-based approach point out that even less than 1 percent of global productivity over a hundred years may translate into considerable suffering and premature death for millions of poor people in vulnerable regions of the less industrialized world.

The issues of risk and justice provide good loci for probing inextricable links between analytic methodologies and underlying social commitments to the Kantian individual in him or herself or the Benthamite aggregate good. Often such issues seem to be intractable when descriptive research and analysis provide the only framework for addressing them.

Typically, policymakers do approach risk characterization as a technical issue: exposure pathways, dose, response, and so on. However, the technical information is unlikely to influence citizens living in an area where environmental risk is present. If the science–policy relationship remains squarely in the descriptive mindset, the response to citizen objections is likely to be the collecting of more technical data; the inclusion of values and worldviews will not be an option. However, if the science–policy relationship is collaborative and includes interpretive data, science will be "more integrated into the policy context, more contextual and openly value-laden, less oriented to mastery over natural and social processes, and more accessible to the public at large" (Robinson 1992a: 249). To the extent that scientists, policymakers, and the public can learn about each other's positions and preferences, the solution space for a problem of risk analysis becomes larger and a solution more possible.

Social science research and policy discourse

In the same way that collaboration is needed between researchers who use descriptive and interpretive approaches, researchers and policymakers need to forge more collaborative relationships. An important element of this collaboration must be the use of both approaches and multiple tools to illuminate many facets of the issues at hand. Current arrangements and policy discourses tend to favor the descriptive approach, although this was not always the case. The policy analysts of the Reformation were the hermeneutic scholars who advised both Catholic and Protestant kings and princes about all aspects of policy based on the interpretation of holy texts and secular precedents.

The descriptive approach to policymaking is usually considered to be more appealing to policymakers because of its immediate potential for instrumental use. Quantitative analyses of responsiveness to tax rates or the effectiveness of regulation can, in principle, be directly translated into a set of policy choices about whether to implement a carbon tax or appliance efficiency standards and even at what level taxes or standards should be set (see "Economic analysis" and "Integrated assessment modeling"). In other words, descriptive research usually manages to come up with a bottom line. Generally, interpretive social science tends to be dismissed by policymakers and their social science advisors as lacking this potential to provide practical guidance. How can social scientists provide powerful, practical research findings sufficiently mindful of research limitations? Can we replace or redefine the model of scientific truth being directly used by policymakers? And what would such a research–policy relationship look like?

First, we can recognize that the model of "speaking truth to power" does not actually mirror the users' reality. Policymakers frequently do not make direct use of descriptive research's bottom lines. Empirical research in the United States (where the instrumentalist emphasis on the bottom line is probably most strongly emphasized) shows that, despite a generally positive attitude to such analysis, it is seldom acted upon in any directly identifiable fashion (Rich 1977, Starling 1979, Weiss & Bucuvalas 1980, Whiteman 1985, House & Shull 1988). These studies indicate that the actual impact of descriptive policy analysis is much more diffuse. Indeed, Weiss (1982) suggests that the real usefulness of policy analysis may lie in enlightenment rather than instrumental purposes, less as a tool for solving specific problems than as a way of orientating themselves toward issues (see "Integrated assessment modeling"). "And much of this is not deliberate, direct, and targeted, but a result of long-term percolation of social science concepts, theories, and findings into the climate of informed opinion" (Weiss 1982: 534). As Heineman et al. put it (1990: 44):

> In summary, instrumental use of policy analysis is not as widespread as analysts would like; however, there is a more diffuse use of policy analysis which can be significant. This use for "enlightenment" is often underplayed in the literature on utilization of policy analysis. . . . If the analyst cannot easily shape a specific policy, his or her findings may still have an impact on the broader policy agenda . . .

The apparent concreteness of descriptive social science information in practice seldom makes it any more usable by decisionmakers for obtaining enlightenment than the results of interpretive studies. Both may contribute equally to the enlightenment of decisionmakers. However, once a course of action is chosen, descriptive data may be more frequently invoked for the purposes of rationalization and persuasion (Patton 1978, Whiteman 1985). Speaking (scientific) truth to (policymaking) power is thus revealed as a coercive illusion worthy of Baum's Wizard of Oz. The answer to "What will we do if we abandon speaking truth to power?" is that "We will do what we have always done but with greater awareness of what we are doing." Abandoning illusions is the first step on the path to authentic empowerment of individuals and communities.

Once that step is taken, we find that paradigms do exist for the relationship of science researchers and policymakers. For example, Robinson, in a series of articles (1982, 1988, 1990, 1991, 1992a) has argued that the "Dragnet" view of science[1] is at the root of "perhaps the most fundamental misconception underlying standard views of the science/policy relationship: that it is a one-way flow of objective information from science to policy" (1982). He proposes instead a model relationship in which researchers, policymakers, and the public form "mutual learning systems" (1992b) that use modeling tools to explore alternative futures ("backcasting") rather than trying to predict the future ("forecasting"). Elements of this model include the explicit recognition that policy questions are not essentially questions of fact but of value, and that both a "physical flows" perspective and an "actor–system" perspective are needed to provide a usefully integrated approach to policy questions (1991).

Such a collaboration would also help researchers and policymakers cope with both uncertainty and ignorance about how the social and biogeophysical systems interact. Indeed, uncertainty about these interactions is of such magnitude as to be better characterized as indeterminacy. Furthermore, this indeterminacy is likely to persist well beyond the timeframe in which actions would need to be taken to prevent, mitigate, or manage potential undesirable aspects of the human–nature interactions.

Making assumptions explicit is essential to make social (and natural) science more relevant and more effective in climate policymaking. When applying a model or theory to a particular situation, the reflexive researcher considers carefully whether or not the assumptions embedded in the approach actually match the policy context in which the knowledge is being used. If they do not, then the information obtained will not be valid for that context; knowledge is thus conditional. Policy decisions that ignore this conditional aspect often meet with strong opposition from people who do not feel that the assumptions are valid for the case at hand (see "Science and decisionmaking"). For example, in democratic societies, if political institutions base their policy decisions on assumptions about human behavior that seem irrelevant to the public's experiences of

---

1. Named for the US television program whose no-nonsense detective hero would prompt witnesses to deliver "Just the facts, ma'am."

itself and the world around it, they risk eroding the very legitimacy they rely upon to implement their policies.

An important effect of a collaboration between a pluralistic social science and policymakers would be the inclusion of social science analyses from the industrializing world. The Southern sensibility has emerged from an experience with weak institutions of governance and with the development project (Appfel Marglin & Marglin 1990, Banuri 1993). Consequently, Southern critics have challenged the modern descriptive features of instrumentalism, impersonality, and legitimization of impersonal violence. Further, the Southern sensibility sees environmentalism as based in an integrated perception of humans and nature, placing emphasis on issues of justice, equity, institutions of governance, and property rights (Banuri & Appfel Marglin 1993). Including these perspectives as data in the climate change debate acknowledges the genuine interdependence of rich and poor nations and broadens the solution space for global policymaking.

The argument at the international level also holds good for the national and local levels of policymaking. Throughout *Human choice and climate change* we have encountered calls for recognition of local knowledge and the engagement of stakeholders in assessing the broadest range of scientific and social issues related to climate change and climate policy. These calls for the creation of what is variously referred to as vernacular, postnormal, or civic science are not merely made out of democratic sentiment, but out of a conviction that the resulting decisions, although not necessarily economically the most efficient, will turn out to be better decisions, judged by a broad range of competing social criteria.

Re-forming the relationship between science research and policymaking would make space for the useful research that exists within interpretive science, for the alternative world views of less industrialized peoples, and for policymaking strategies that account for uncertainty and indeterminacy. The science and policy community would then include needs, wants, and beliefs in its datasets, alongside measurements and statistics. Policy agreements would explicitly include social organization data and cultural assumptions, as well as market and consumption data, to make them more implementable and effective.

The social science tools and methods that have played the most visible roles in climate change debates have been cost–benefit analysis and risk and decisionmaking frameworks based on the rational actor paradigm. These are descriptive tools that have great explanatory power within a strict set of assumptions that includes complete information and unfettered markets. Because they are limited in this way, they cannot tell the whole story, cannot provide a clear roadmap to the future. Other tools and methods are available within the social sciences, but they have not been tried and tested for their worth to policymakers. Social scientists have the opportunity in the global climate change debate to develop tools—perhaps an integrated set of interpretive and descriptive tools—that can contribute understanding and practical guidance to policymakers.

References

Appfel Marglin, F. & S. A. Marglin (eds) 1990. *Dominating knowledge*, Oxford: Oxford University Press.

Banuri, T. 1993. The landscape of diplomatic conflicts. In *Global ecology: a new arena of political conflict*, W. Sachs (ed.). London: Zed Books.
Banuri, T. & F. Appfel Marglin 1993. *Who will save the forests?* London: Zed Books.
Bullard, R. D. 1994. Unequal environmental protection: incorporating environmental justice in decision making. See Finkel & Golding (1994).

Clark, W. C. 1986. Who cares about climate change? *Environment* **28**(8), 1.
Castri, F. di 1989. Enhancing the credibility of ecology: is interdisciplinary research for land use planning useful? *Geojournal* **13**, 229–325.

Damasio, A. R. 1994. *Descartes' error: emotion, reason, and the human brain*. New York: Putnam.
Douglas, M. & S. Ney 1998. *Missing persons: personhood in the social sciences*. Berkeley: University of California Press.

Edelman, G. M. 1994. *Bright air, brilliant fire: on the matter of the mind*. New York: Basic Books.

Finkel, A. & D. Golding 1994. *Worst things first: the debate over risk-based national environmental priorities*. Washington DC: Resources for the Future.
Fish, S. 1994. *There's no such thing as free speech (and it's a good thing, too)*. New York: Oxford University Press.

Geertz, C. 1973. *The interpretation of culture*. New York: Basic Books.
Gross, J. & S. Rayner 1985. *Measuring culture: a paradigm for the analysis of social organization*. New York: Columbia University Press.
Gudeman, S. 1986. *Economics as culture: models and metaphors of livelihood*. London: Routledge & Kegan Paul.

Hannerz, U. 1986. Theory in anthropology: small is beautiful? The problems of complex culture. *Comparative Studies in Society and History* **28**(2), 362–7.
Headrick, D. R. 1990. Technological change. See Turner et al. (1990a).
Heineman, R. A., W. T. Bluhm, S. A. Peterson, E. N. Kearny 1990. *The world of the policy analyst: rationality, values, and politics*. Chatham, New Jersey: Chatham House Publishers.
House, P. W. & R. D. Shull 1988. *Rush to policy*. New Brunswick, New Jersey: Transaction.

Ingold, T. 1993. Globes and spheres: the topology of environmentalism. In *The view from anthropology*, K. Milton (ed.). London: Routledge.

Koford, K. J. & J. B. Miller 1991. Habit, custom and norms in economics. In *Social norms and economic institutions*, K. J. Koford & J. B. Miller (eds). Ann Arbor: University of Michigan Press.

Kuhn, T. S. 1970. *The structure of scientific revolutions*, 2nd edn. Chicago: University of Chicago Press.

Latour, B. 1986. Visualization and cognition: thinking with eyes and hands. *Knowledge and Society: Studies in the Sociology of Culture, Past and Present* **6**, 1–40.

Lavine, T. Z. 1984. *From Socrates to Sartre: the philosophical quest*. New York: Bantam Books.

Locke, J. 1690. *An essay concerning human understanding*. London: T. Basset. [Reprinted in 1990, together with a facsimile of the most extensive additions in the 2nd edn, by Scolar Press, Aldershot, England.]

Lutz, W. (ed.) 1996. *The future population of the world: what can we assume today?* London: Earthscan.

Malinowski, B. 1944. *A scientific theory of culture*. Chapel Hill: University of North Carolina Press.

Malone, T. F. 1985. Preface. In *Global change*, T. F. Malone & J. G. Roederer (eds). Cambridge: Cambridge University Press.

Merchant, C. 1990. The realm of social relations: production, reproduction, and gender in environmental transformations. See Turner et al. (1990a).

Nichols, A. L. 1994. Risk-based priorities and environmental justice. See Finkel & Golding (1994).

Patton, M. Q. 1978. *Utilization focused evaluation*. Beverly Hills, California: Sage.

Quesnay, F. 1758. *Tableau économique*. [Translated and edited by M. Kuczynski & R. L. Meek as *Quesnay's Tableau économique*, London: Macmillan, 1972.]

Radcliffe-Brown, A. R. 1957. *A natural science of society*. Glencoe, Illinois: Free Press.

Ricardo, D. 1814 (1952). *The works and correspondence of David Ricardo* [edited by P. Sraffa]. Cambridge: Cambridge University Press.

Rich, R. F. 1977. Uses of social science information by federal bureaucracies. In *Using social research in public policy making*, C. H. Weiss (ed.). Lexington, Massachusetts: Lexington Press.

Robinson, J. B. 1982. Apples and horned toads: on the framework-determined nature of the energy debate. *Policy Sciences* **15**, 23–45.

——1988. Unlearning and backcasting: rethinking some of the questions we ask about the future. *Technological Forecasting and Social Change* **33**, 325–38.

——1990. Futures under glass: a recipe for people who hate to predict. *Futures* **22** (9), 820–43.

——1991. Modelling the interactions between human and natural systems. *Global Environmental Change* **1**(November), 629–47.

——1992a. Of maps and territories: the use and abuse of socioeconomic modeling in support of decision making. *Technological Forecasting and Social Change* **42**, 147–64.

——1992b. Risks, predictions, and other optical illusions: rethinking the use of science in social decision-making. *Policy Sciences* **25**, 237–54.

Robinson, J. B. & P. Timmerman 1993. Myths, rules, artifacts, and ecosystems: framing the human dimensions of global change. In *Human ecology: crossing boundaries*, S. D. Wright, T. Dietz, R. Borden, G. Young, G. Guagnano (eds). Fort Collins, Colorado: Society for Human Ecology.

Russell, B. 1946. *History of Western philosophy*. London: George Allen & Unwin.

Ryle, G. 1949. *The concept of mind*. London: Hutchinson.

Schneider, S. 1987. An international program on global change, can it endure? *Climatic Change* **10**, 11–18.

Selznick, P. 1992. *The moral commonwealth: social theory and the promise of continuity*. Berkeley: University of California Press.

Snow, C. P. 1959. *The two cultures*. Cambridge: Cambridge University Press.

Starling, G. 1979. *The politics and economics of public policy*. Homewood, Illinois: Dorsey Press.

Turner II, B. L., W. C. Clark, R. W. Kates, J. F. Richards, J. T. Mathews, W. B. Meyer (eds) 1990a. *The Earth transformed by human action: global and regional changes in the biosphere over the past 300 years*. Cambridge: Cambridge University Press.

Turner II, B. L., R. E. Kasperson, W. B. Meyer, K. M. Dow, D. Golding, J. X. Kasperson, R. C. Mitchell, S. J. Ratick 1990b. Two types of environmental change: definitional and spatial-scale issues in their human dimensions. *Global Environmental Change* 1(1), 14–21.

United Nations 1992. *Framework Convention on Climate Change*. New York: United Nations.

Watson, R. T., M. C. Zinyowera, R. H. Moss (eds) 1996. *Climate change 1995: impacts, adaptations, and mitigation*. Cambridge: Cambridge University Press.

Weiss, C. H. 1982. Policy research in the context of diffuse decision-making. In *Social science research and public policy-making*, D. B. P. Kallen (ed.). Windsor: NFER–Nelson.

Weiss, C. H., & M. J. Bucuvalas 1980. Truth tests and utility tests. *American Sociological Review* 45, 302–313.

Whiteman, D. 1985. The fate of policy analysis in Congressional decision-making. *Western Political Quarterly* 38, 294–311.

69

CHAPTER 3

Social science insights into climate change

Steve Rayner & Elizabeth L. Malone

Contributors
Chester L. Cooper, James A. Edmonds

From the methodological challenges that climate change and other large complex issues present to the intellectual organization of the social sciences and their analytical tools, we now return to the social science insights into climate change. In Chapter 1 we listed a sample of questions about how humans exercise choice in relation to understanding, causing, and responding to climate change. Although these are by no means exhaustive, they represent a sufficiently broad cross-section of issues upon which to assess the current state of social science knowledge about human choice and climate change. To recap, the questions are:

- How do scientists choose to study climate change? How do they form a scientific consensus?
- How do people decide that climate change is worthy of attention?
- How do people attribute blame for climate change and choose solutions?
- How do people choose whom to believe about climate change and at what level of risk do they or should they choose to act?
- How do people and institutions mobilize support for (or against) policy action on climate change?
- What is the relationship between resource management choices and climate change?
- How do governments establish where climate change stands in relation to other political priorities? How do they choose the climate change issues around which to formulate goals?
- How are climate change policy instruments chosen?
- Why and how did the international community choose to address climate change?
- How do societies select technologies that cause, mitigate, or assist adaptation to climate change?
- How can research on social or collective action be useful to the global climate change debate?

In this chapter we, the editors of *Human choice and climate change*, draw upon the work of our authors and contributors to see what kind of light the social sciences can shed upon questions such as these. In so doing, we elucidate what we regard as some of the most significant crosscutting themes of the assessment, although we do not claim to be exhaustive. Readers can find the fuller arguments and supporting data in the appropriate chapters, where there is much more information to be mined than we can possibly summarize here. Our goal is to summarize what social science has to say about global climate change and the debates that surround it, and how this information can be used both to set the future research agenda and to inform the policy process. However, we reserve actual suggestions to policymakers for the final chapter.

How do scientists choose to study climate change?
How do they form a scientific consensus?

Contemporary science and technology studies suggest that the issue of climate change, like other global environmental issues, has emerged from an interplay among scientific and political agendas. "Science and decision-making" describes how scientific knowledge and political order are routinely co-produced at multiple stages in their joint evolution, from the moment when scientific findings are stabilized in laboratories and field studies to the time when nations and international institutions accept the explanations offered by science for use in decisionmaking. This process of co-production does not invalidate scientific findings, but it does tend to invest science for policy with a Janus-like character. On the one hand, scientific knowledge, even in the physical sciences and mathematics, develops through significant processes of social negotiation and consensus building. On the other hand, policymakers, scientists, and lay publics all share an explicit commitment to the idea of science as objective—providing value-free facts to policymakers in a kind of black box whose origins cannot be discerned. For example, "In American politics there is constant pressure to convert political questions into technical questions, so that they can be referred to experts without actually confronting the value differences that frequently are the real origin of conflict" (Brooks 1976: 244). The same process can be seen at work on a global scale in the case of climate change.

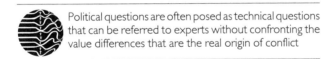

Political questions are often posed as technical questions that can be referred to experts without confronting the value differences that are the real origin of conflict

Scientific consensus about climate change has been built through strategic alliances among those investigating a variety of processes and topics to frame an "Earth systems science." This alliance has matured through the creation of scientific advisory committees, by the standardization of inquiry (most notably in computer models), and pre-eminently by the processes of the Intergovernmental Panel on Climate Change (IPCC). These are the means by which scientific knowledge and practices become standardized and widely accepted. Scientific internationalism is not simply a matter of cooperation across existing research agendas. International institutions also produce new forms of knowledge, beliefs, and political action; they are not just passive facilitators of convergence toward an independently optimal end-point of international bargaining.

Scientific advisory committees in general offer a powerful way to legitimize knowledge claims. For climate change, the IPCC has played this role, providing a great deal of agreed-upon knowledge and criteria for evaluating "good" science to nations, other institutions (e.g., environment-focused nongovernmental organizations), and citizens in many parts of the world. "Institutions for political action" describes how the IPCC process has made a significant contribution to building trust and confidence among the participating nations—a process just as important as providing a common scientific basis for negotiations.

However, the process of establishing an authoritative voice for science also has its downside. As consensus is formed, issues necessarily become more narrowly framed, and this narrowing can lead to sharp controversies. A considerable body of social science research has illuminated the origins of controversy and uncertainty in public policy. Given the prominence accorded by the media to backlash critiques of climate change science, this line of inquiry will likely grow in importance as policymakers confront the challenge of international cooperation. Trust is a crucial issue: public trust in science and scientists, citizens' trust in their states, states' trust in other states' good intentions and in the international science–policy process. But the terms under which trust is established may vary widely around the world. Science in North America, for example, is exposed to skeptical review; intense scrutiny of scientific claims is routine in litigation, and technical debate often takes the place of political consensus building. Such performance-based trust contrasts with those societies where trust is based on the status or position of individuals or on processes of cooperative consensus building.

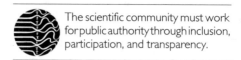

The scientific community must work for public authority through inclusion, participation, and transparency.

By casting its net of presumed cognitive and predictive control over ever more complex and dispersed phenomena, the scientific study of climate change may generate expectations that cannot be met and promises that may begin to strike many as illusory. The political backlash in the United States against the ozone agreements and against the emerging scientific consensus on global warming may be an indication that the scientific and science–policy consensus is not strong enough to prompt action.

To avoid promoting unrealistic public and policymaker expectations of scientific prediction and control over nature, the scientific community investigating climate change must work for acceptance and public authority through patiently constructing communities of belief that provide legitimacy through inclusion, participation, and transparency.

How do people decide that climate change is worthy of attention?

Research on public concerns about climate change has led to two main results. The first is that global climate change has become a concern not just among experts but also among lay people. US figures reveal that between 1982 and 1989 the percentage of people believing the "greenhouse effect" to be a "very serious problem" increased by roughly 30 percent. The second is that lay people confuse global warming with other environmental problems such as ozone depletion. But how do we explain the existence of public concern? If it is the result of people's encounter with scientific information, how do we reconcile the high level of expressed concern with apparent confusion over the causes and impacts of climate change and the apparent absence of, even opposition to, widespread behavioral change to reduce human impacts on the atmosphere?

Recent surveys have shown that public support for environmental protection is strong, particularly in the industrialized countries where there is an expressed willingness to pay for products that do not harm the environment. Many people say they have witnessed the deterioration of their local environments in their lifetimes and therefore have a direct experience of environmental problems. In the same vein, concern for the local environment and for personal health is an important factor in support for local environmental protection schemes. Such observations fit well with what is called the *knowledge-based approach*, the assumption that people worry about the things that are worth worrying about: a commonsense assumption which, as analyzed in "Cultural discourses" does not hold up well.

A different approach sees the rising curve of environmental concern as stemming from changes in ethical frameworks. One of these, the *postmaterialism* explanation, relies on the concept of a hierarchy of needs in which individuals and societies that have their basic needs for food, shelter, security, and education can then spare time to worry about the environment. However, "Human needs and wants" gives us reason to be wary of such explanations, pointing out that the *ethical-shift* explanation represents an uncaused cause: no explanation at all. Efforts to combine the knowledge-based and ethical-shift approaches seem to be susceptible to the criticisms leveled at both.

Survey research has revealed that people have *mental models* of the environment in general and climate change in particular. Kempton (1991: 193) concludes that "we have a historical propensity to perceive weather change, whether or not it is occurring, and to attribute it to human perturbations." The present publicity and scientific concern about global climate change therefore comport with the lay propensity to attribute changes in weather patterns to human activity, and it is this combination, Kempton et al. (1995: 85) suggest, that explains why "a potentially implausible hypothesis—that human activities will

warm the entire planet—has been so readily picked up by the general public."
Nor, we should note, is it safe to assume, as the expert/lay distinctions of the
knowledge-based approach encourages us to assume, that this propensity is
confined to lay people. Houghton—the eminent British scientist who chairs the
IPCC Working Group I—even goes a step further and sees the catastrophes that
are about to befall us as divine retribution. In any case, if different people use
different mental models or the same people use different ones at different times,
we are left with the question of where mental models come from.

 People know what they know because of whom they know. The shape of
social networks, rather than the form and volume of information, seems
to be the key variable in whether people pay attention to climate change.

Membership of institutions, communities, and looser-knit social networks—
all forms of *social solidarity*—shapes people's sensitivities to risk in general and
threats to environmental and climate change in particular. This explanation centers on the need to hold together something shared. It does not require that the
environment actually be getting worse (only the shared perception that it is or
may be), nor does it have to invoke a value shift (an uncaused cause) from
anthropocentrism to ecocentrism. It also holds out the possibility of explaining
why it is that not everyone shares the same concerns. The explanation that people know what they know because of whom they know is consistent with work
on risk perception, such as that of Kunreuther et al. (1978) who found that the
only statistically significant factor that explained people's purchase of flood
disaster insurance was knowing someone else who already had it.

In the only direct empirical comparison of approaches we could find that was
designed to test the knowledge-based, ethical shift, and sociocultural (social
solidarity) approaches, the knowledge-based approach fared worst, the ethical
shift fared better, and the sociocultural approach fared best. This research result
would go a long way toward explaining why public information campaigns do
so poorly at increasing public awareness of climate change and altering people's
behavior. The shape of social networks, rather than the form and volume of
information, seems to be the key variable in whether people pay attention to
climate change.

How do people attribute blame for climate change and choose solutions?

When people decide that an issue is worthy of attention, they join that issue to their knowledge bases, mental models, and their views of nature and society (what is natural and what is right); these elements are inextricably entwined with their social networks. Out of this complex social web emerge various accountings of the climate change issue. "Cultural discourses" identifies three candidate causes for climate change that emerge in public debates, each with its own solution.

Population

Increasing population is often cited as the underlying cause of climate change. The argument goes that, if we had fewer people, they would use fewer resources and thus would emit lower amounts (maybe very little) of greenhouse gases. However, "Population and health" shows that institutional arrangements for habitation, agricultural production, and other aspects of social life are the critical factors in how much pressure an increasing population puts on the environment. The number of people, in and of itself, does not cause climate change.

Institutional arrangements are the critical factors in how much pressure population puts on the environment. The number of people, in and of itself, does not cause climate change.

Increasing population means, among other considerations, increased pressure on scarce resources and environmental stresses. But, again, resource and environmental problems do not result from aggregate population growth in itself, but from local conditions such as overcrowding, poor public health systems and other infrastructural inadequacies, and indiscriminate use of local resources. The example of the Netherlands shows that high population density does not inevitably lead to environmental devastation, whereas the case of Hong Kong illustrates that high fertility and rapid population growth do not inevitably mire nations in poverty. With that caveat in mind, population projections remain an important element of the future world.

Certainly the number of people on Earth is increasing and will continue to increase. Based on the present age composition and fertility/mortality trends, demographers are reasonably certain that the world's population will continue to grow (to between 8.1 and 12.0 billion by 2050), its distribution will continue to tilt from highly industrialized to less industrialized countries, and it will continue to age.

The principal uncertainty in the long-term demographic outlook is the speed and extent of the decline in fertility rates now underway in less industrialized countries, presumably a stage in the demographic transition already experienced in more industrialized countries. The effects from this fertility decline will not be felt in the short term because of demographic inertia. Long-term trends are based on well-developed demographic methodologies, derived from a set of identities involving fertility, mortality, and net migration. Of these three factors, fertility is the most important determinant of population size. However, fertility rates are not easy to predict; fertility decline is complex, regionally differentiated, and context dependent, involving synergies among family planning programs, decreases in poverty, and empowerment of women.

 At the global, aggregate level, climate change may not have an appreciable impact on mortality, fertility, and immigration, nor on global GNP. The population debate is as much about values as it is about physical limits to sustainability.

At the global, aggregate level, climate change may not have an appreciable impact on mortality, fertility, and immigration, nor on global GNP. However, at the regional and local levels, among populations that are poor and therefore underrepresented in GNP figures, climate change may have severe impacts.

Important uncertainties arise from possible political, cultural, and other institutional changes, as well as changes in the ability of the environment to support humans (positive and negative changes) and possible health and mortality changes. Institutional issues are largely questions of value, and, as the authors of "Population and health" conclude, the population debate is as much about values as it is about physical limits to sustainability.

Consumption

This brings us to another often-cited cause of climate change, human energy use and land use, often lumped together under the term "consumption." Energy production, transformation, and consumption constitute the largest single source of anthropogenic emissions of greenhouse-related gases. Further, as reported in "Energy and industry," energy use has grown and evolved substantially in the past two centuries, with enormous changes in scale and shifts from wood to coal to oil. Similarly, land-use change has contributed as much to the atmospheric increase of carbon dioxide over the course of human history as has fossil fuel combustion. Moreover, land use is the leading source of methane and a major source of nitrous oxide, two potent greenhouse gases. Land and water have two other functions in climate change:

- Land-use activities are important emitters, through biomass burning, of aerosols, which can lessen net radiative forcing.

- Plants, animals, soils, and oceans act as reservoirs for carbon; the first three now hold almost three times the amount of carbon that is in the atmosphere.

As consumption, human activities related to energy and land use are generally agreed to be contributing to an increasing greenhouse effect that will result in climatic changes. Efforts to satisfy human wants and needs, in a sense, underlie this whole issue. Family and lifestyle shape population patterns and deplete natural resources. Aspirations to live well influence the selection of technologies and the rate of their penetration. The principal means for satisfying needs and wants through technology and economic activity depend upon energy use (especially in the industrialized world) and land use (especially in the less industrialized world).

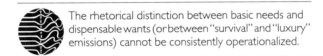

The rhetorical distinction between basic needs and dispensable wants (or between "survival" and "luxury" emissions) cannot be consistently operationalized.

As reported in "Needs and wants," social science has failed to find an operational distinction between so-called basic needs and dispensable wants (or between "survival" and "luxury" emissions) that is sustainable in practice. The needs theories that provide hierarchies of individual needs (stratified in such a way that each level requires satisfaction before a person can attend to the next) prove problematic upon examination. Prepotency is not clear-cut; there are no sharp target levels after which one urge disappears and the next suddenly appears. Needs are complementary, and transition may be gradual. Research finds much co-occurrence of needs. These findings call into question attempts to base environmental policies on a hierarchy of basic needs and derived wants, for example, proposals to allocate emissions rights preferentially to what are labelled "survival" rather than "luxury" emissions.

Merging needs and wants and accounting for them in the goods that allow people to take and maintain their places in society provide a more realistic analysis of consumption. Analysts and policymakers can then see why it is difficult for people from different societies to agree about what emissions are necessary in other societies. This difficulty is intensified by the contrast between worldviews that represent nature as a controllable means to satisfy human needs and wants and those worldviews that represent nature and humans as inseparable, neither controlling the other. It is further complicated by the view that the environment has needs independent of—perhaps opposed to—human needs. Needs theories are focused on protecting humans, whereas the Framework Convention on Climate Change (FCCC) focuses on the "need" to protect the climate from human activities that will change it. That is, we cannot prior-itize the environment within a framework of individual needs; neither an envi-ronmental nor a consumptive imperative can be justified on first principles.

Societies and tastes are produced reciprocally. As people try to form a kind of society, they formulate wants and needs they are going to consider acceptable and set themselves to procure what will satisfy those wants and needs. What matters is to discover the system of feedbacks in this process. If people want an unpolluted environment, they will change their laws and customs, and chang-ing these will change the pattern of wealth and income distribution, and this will change the targeted flows of goods and services.

Even with this improved analysis of wants and consumption, however, we still face a fundamental disagreement in the subject of global change, as described in "Economic analysis": whether environmental protection is at odds with an economic approach committed to perpetual growth or whether halting climate change would require immense resources that can only be raised by continued economic growth.

Prices and property rights

The focus on the price mechanism and property rights essentially views climate change as a technical problem requiring adjustments to ownership and trading arrangements that will enhance the efficient operation of markets. This kind of approach to climate change tends to dominate the field described in "Economic analysis." The prices and property rights diagnosis sees the climate debate in terms of scarcity and costs. Historically, market prices have not accurately reflected the full social cost of natural resources. As a result, scarce natural resources, such as the atmosphere, the world's forests, and the seas, have been overutilized to the brink of exhaustion. This diagnosis identifies distorted resource prices, usually resulting from misguided economic policy, as the prime culprit. From this point of view, market failures occur because technol-ogy is not priced correctly, that is, prices fail to includes environmental costs. Although advocates of this view often present their arguments in equations, it is a strongly normative view that places a high value on efficiency as a moral imperative underlying the rational calculus. Even where the normative content of the climate debate is acknowledged, this diagnosis argues that a successful climate policy can be implemented by technical adjustments to existing insti-tutions.

As the authors of "Cultural discourses" point out, the diagnosis implies its own solution. Unlike the proposed solution to present consumption patterns— less consumption—a market-based problem implies a market solution. First,

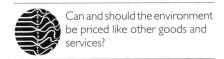
Can and should the environment be priced like other goods and services?

policymakers devise ways to incorporate the true environmental costs into consumer products (broadly defined to include environmental goods such as the wilderness and biodiversity) and allocate property rights so everyone has a stake in preserving the environment or making sustainable use of it. If these policies are in place, demand will shift toward environmentally sustainable products and services. People will make appropriate tradeoffs with other priorities.

However, extending market concepts and structures to environmental goods (and bads) raises many difficult issues in accounting, as well as a basic issue about whether the environment should be priced like other goods and services; these issues are discussed in "Economic analysis" and "Cultural discourses." Depending upon the implied discount rate that they are using, for example, some stakeholders could well decide that the cost of maintaining biodiversity is too high. Such a conclusion would be unacceptable to other significant stakeholder groups.

If each diagnosis is wrong, what's right?

All three diagnoses represent partial explanations. The problem is not so much that any one is entirely wrong and none is entirely right, as that each pulls policymakers in different directions that cannot be resolved by analytic agility or a neat technocratic trick. When confronted by such a dilemma, stepping back to examine alternative framings of the problem and solution can be a fruitful endeavor.

The populations most adversely affected will be poor and marginal populations in less industrialized countries who depend on ecologically fragile renewable natural resources.

A major result of the debate among the three viewpoints has been to divert attention from the important issue of coping with climate change. Obscured almost entirely in the debate is one of the most consistent findings to emerge from climate change research: that the populations most adversely affected will be poor and marginal populations in less industrialized countries who depend on ecologically fragile renewable natural resources. They are the least likely to reduce family sizes, since large families are essential to individual, household, and cultural survival. They are already frugal. And their market power is negligible. The truly vulnerable are left out of the debate altogether. Only by focusing on means of adaptation can the needs of the seriously affected populations be addressed.

Furthermore, by trying to fix blame on each other, the population, consumption, and pricing diagnoses all fail to recognize their mutual interrelations. The causes of climate change involve population and consumption and the technological means by which the consumption of that population is satisfied. The interactions among humans, economic growth, and technology produce emissions. Future emissions are much more sensitive to changes in per capita emissions associated with economic growth, structural change, and technological progress than to changes in fertility and mortality rates. Policymakers need to address all of these human dimensions, not as separate problems, but as interrelated elements, to design effective interventions. In other words, a broad social science perspective suggests that climate change is not a problem that can be fixed in isolation from other social and ecological commitments. It may be better approached as just one issue in an interlocking challenge of how to achieve sustainable human development.

How do people choose whom to believe about climate change and at what level of risk do they and should they choose to act?

According to the most commonly applied social science model of decision-making, the rational choice perspective, decisionmakers (particularly in the private sector) are strongly motivated, by the desire to optimize performance. They therefore readily incorporate research results and price information into their decisionmaking. Failure to incorporate such information is characterized as an exogenous barrier or remediable market imperfection.

 .Identifying opportunities to introduce information into real-world decision processes may be a more effective policy strategy than trying to make decision processes conform more closely to the rational choice model.

However, sociological studies suggest that information in organizations and institutions of all kinds is not a well-behaved commodity that can be passed between parties like water poured from one bucket to another. The use of information in institutions and organizations is inextricably bound up with creating collective meaning and identity as well as servicing implicit goals of organizational maintenance that are not captured by applications of the rational choice model. The sociological perspective proposed in "Cultural discourses,"

"Energy and society," and "Decision analysis" suggests that identifying opportunities to introduce information into real-world decision processes may be a more effective policy strategy than trying to make decision processes conform more closely to the rational choice model.

The communication of information depends crucially upon several factors. People's views of nature and society govern what they can hear and how they interpret it. Their shared-meaning networks similarly bound the types of information that can be communicated and the significance of the information. When information comes from other sources, they will evaluate the source of the information (What is the level of trust that can be placed in the source?) as much as or more than the information itself.

With respect to the issue of risk, "Economic analysis" describes how damage assessments have computed the costs of climate change impacts (either as a set or singly, e.g., the costs of sea level rise) in various ways, usually expressed as a bottom-line percentage of global (or national) gross domestic product (GDP). This percentage varies by region; the IPCC report cites estimates of between 1 and 2 percent for industrialized countries and between 2 and 9 percent for less industrialized countries. These estimates, of course, rest on "a number of simplifying and often controversial assumptions" (Pearce et al. 1996), for example, the value of a human life. Such best-guess estimates will presumably help policymakers to perform appropriate tradeoffs among other priorities. But choices among policy priorities are not solely—many social scientists would argue, not primarily—matters of dollar-denominated cost–benefit analysis.

Risk responsiveness is an institutional judgment, even for individuals.

Given the uncertainties in cost estimates and the lack of a holistic tradeoff analysis, neither researchers nor policymakers know what the costs of coping with climate change are. We do know that the way the issues are currently framed does not lead to resolution. Many social costs and benefits are not accounted for in the decisionmaking methods, with their overemphasis on linear rationality (discussed in "Decision analysis"). Probably policymakers are missing the real win–wins that could be identified in a broader discussion that includes quality and meaning issues. In the final analysis, risk responsiveness is an institutional judgment, even for individuals.

How do people and institutions mobilize support for (or against) policy action on climate change?

"Institutions for political action" makes it clear that mobilizing support for actions to mitigate or adapt to climate change involves bringing diverse lay publics to a consensus that specific actions are required. We have already mentioned that recent surveys, summarized in "Cultural discourses," show that, although public support for environmental protection is strong and global climate change is identified as a concern, lay people display confusion about the facts and dynamics of climate change, tending to confuse it with ozone depletion and other environmental problems.

However, knowledge deficiencies are not the point. Information relevant to lay publics addresses relationships between humans and nature, and takes into account different views of nature—as robust, fragile, or robust within limits. These different views are connected with different cultural biases and different policy preferences. Often the differences cannot be reconciled, because each group defines itself in contradistinction to the others. Recognizing the differences in views provides a realistic perspective from which to participate in debate with a heightened ability to listen to and understand the arguments and standpoints of other participants, as well as to be aware of the role played by one's own institutional bias.

On a global scale, understanding these differences is crucially important to designing effective policy. Formulating overall goals related to the environment and providing multiple strategies for meeting those goals comprise an approach to accommodating diverse value sets within a framework for mobilization.

Policymakers, like other people, cannot agree on a best equity principle.

Also important are the issues that have been joined to climate change as global institutions consider possible policy actions. Nonscientists tend to couple the climate change issue with other issues about the disturbed relationship of humans and nature. Those concerned about potential problems of an increasing population join that issue to climate change, since the causes of climate change are anthropocentric and emissions-producing activities are projected to increase along with population. Others connect the desire to reduce consumption, that is, to adopt a simpler lifestyle, with the climate change concern about increasing emissions. The problems of poverty, neocolonialism, debt, low status of women, and weak institutions of governance have all been conjoined to climate change issues—and, indeed, each has a connection with climate change.

Equity is a crucially important issue associated with climate change. Disagreements about the "problem" of climate change and the appropriate actions are compounded when viewed through the lens of equity. Further, improving scientific information about the uneven geographical distribution of costs resulting from regional impacts of climate change may exacerbate rather than facilitate the search for a fair international solution.

Climate change provides an arena for debating a wide variety of social, economic, and political issues that societies find difficult to address directly.

"Cultural discourses" describes three principles that can be applied to resolve practical problems of making fair allocations of resources: proportionality, priority, and parity. The proportionality argument attempts to combine both population and GDP in a compromise formula for allocating emissions rights. Priority gives a first-in-time preference; thus, a fair allocation of emissions rights would be based on GDP. Parity means that each inhabitant of the Earth has the right to an equal use of the atmosphere; hence, a fair allocation of emissions rights would be based on per capita population.

But policymakers, like other people, cannot agree on a best equity principle. And much of the debate about equity in climate change mitigation is an extension of the broader debate about international economic development and political empowerment.

Climate change provides an arena for debating a wide variety of social, economic, and political issues that societies find difficult to address directly. This may be an important opportunity for mobilizing social action on many issues— or the costs of debating significant social and economic change in a surrogate arena may reduce our capacity to make desirable changes.

What is the relationship between resource management choices and climate change?

Human choice and climate change gives a representative picture of a broad spread of quantitative and qualitative knowledge, information, and insight related to resource management issues. These issues are relevant to human activities that contribute to climate change and will be affected by climate change or policies designed to prevent or ameliorate its impacts on human populations. "Land and water use," "Coastal zones and oceans," "Energy and industry," and "Reasoning by analogy" all explore the issues surrounding human uses of land, water, and energy; sociocultural differences in various resource use patterns; and how and why humans might change these behaviors. To a certain extent, our findings overlap with those of the IPCC, which included a selection of social science findings (principally those from economics) in its Second Assessment Report (Bruce et al. 1996, Watson et al. 1996). Some examples of common findings are presented in Box 3.1. However, starting with a social science orientation, we have been able to extend the reach of the assessment to garner insights from the full range of disciplinary and interdisciplinary research.

Land and water use

The links among climate, natural resource use, and economic well-being are ancient. Agriculture, forestry, and other land uses for human activities have been affected by climate; indeed, the notion that climate determined human activities and social structures was current into the twentieth century. Although linking climate, natural resources, and economics is not new, the modern potential for humans to affect the climate because of the large scale of economic activities prompts researchers to study the nature of the link closely. Current research emphasizes climate–human interactions. Indeed, one of the most conspicuous examples of successful collaboration between the social and natural sciences on the issue of climate and other global environmental changes is that of researchers on land use and land cover during the 1990s. People's uses of land and water always interact with natural processes; in turn, biophysical processes constrain or facilitate human uses. Land tenure systems, land and water rights, and institutional supports for agriculture complicate the picture of land and water use.

Socioeconomic changes will be much more rapid and significant than climate change in the foreseeable future.

Land use and water use occupy a central position in the issue of climate change, not least because land-use change represents an important source of greenhouse-related emissions—0.7 to 2.6 petagrams of carbon per year. Cultivated land area is currently estimated at about 15 million km^2. Sixteen percent of this cultivated land is irrigated; fertilizer use has increased globally by 19 percent over the past decade. Principal alterations that contribute to climate change include deforestation (although North America is undergoing reforestation, while other regions are being deforested), settlement increase, and wetland decrease.

A recurrent theme in land and water research includes possible tradeoffs between high management capacity and high response flexibility, especially in light of the likelihood that socioeconomic changes will be much more rapid and significant than climate change in the foreseeable future. Past increases in output based on homogeneous crops and high fertilization rates may need to be altered to provide more resilient strategies (e.g., intercropping and precision application of fertilizers) to increase farmers' ability to respond to climate changes. A related focus is the variety of levels at which adaptive responses can take place, and the importance of developing multipurpose no-regrets options for land and water management with or without climate change.

Land tenure systems are an important consideration in evaluating potential land-use changes and policy interventions; similarly, different systems for assigning water rights (especially internationally) complicate questions of effective policy. Land tenure systems and the cultural differences that spawn them limit changes that can be made, but the same systems may provide resilience and flexibility. Although no particular system of property rights (private, common, and so forth) is inherently superior, the failure of forest management in less industrialized countries is often the result of poor or contested definition of property rights. In a comparable way, disputes over fishing rights may allow overfishing to continue.

Important constraints, involving economics, politics, culture, and equity, may make policy measures designed to improve resource use infeasible even though they may appear technically and even financially irreproachable. Constraints include:

- entrenched support for agricultural production
- reliance of much of the world's population on agriculture for subsistence and livelihood
- nonassignment of property rights to traditional, sustainable use of forests
- labor and capital constraints on potential users of low-emitting techniques
- secondary effects and leakage (the potential for perverse effects, for example, a change to reduce emissions that increases emissions at another site).

One focal point for studying human activities is coastal zone regions. Two-thirds of the world's people live in coastal zones, including a large proportion of subsistence economies (fishing and farming). The big losers from global climate change, especially if significant sea level rise is a consequence, are most likely to be small island nations and poor countries with large, densely populated, low-lying coastal areas, whereas industrialized nations may be able to protect or adapt relatively easily. Disaster research indicates that natural disasters in coastal areas (e.g., cyclones) cause economic damage in industrialized

Box 3.1   Resource-use findings common to the IPCC and *Human choice and climate change*

The IPCC Second Assessment Report and *Human choice and climate change* converge on several findings that are significant with respect to climate change and resource use:
- The prospect for continued increases in scale implies continued increases in the emission of greenhouse-related gases; although these increases are likely, they are not guaranteed.
- The range of future fossil-fuel carbon emissions is expected to more than double over the course of the next century, but projections differ by more than an order of magnitude.
- The simultaneous emissions of sulfur and carbon in energy use significantly complicate the search for an optimal policy response. Sulfur emissions have cooling effects, which mitigate the warming effects of carbon dioxide and other greenhouse gases.
- The resource base of fossil fuels places no meaningful constraint on loading carbon into the atmosphere, although available conventional oil and gas are presently thought to be insufficient to effect a doubling of the preindustrial concentration of atmospheric carbon dioxide.
- Agriculture is potentially vulnerable, and local societies might have problems adjusting, even if total agricultural output were unchanged but the distribution of production changed.
- The extent to which agriculture in less industrialized nations will be affected is widely disputed. In one view, these nations lack technical and social systems that will cushion shocks. Another view is that conventional assumptions about vulnerability of agriculture in less industrialized nations need to be offset by recognizing its greater diversity and adaptivity.
- Health could be affected by heat, but disease is potentially more important (although total numbers of people will not likely be affected).
- Environmental security could be important if climate change-related stresses such as migration destabilize already precarious international relationships.
- The real potential for harm lies in surprise.
- Global climate change, experienced as regional climate change, will affect human water uses already putting stresses on the environment, particularly irrigation and displacement (e.g., for hydropower, a non-emitting technology)
- Addition of climate change further complicates situations about which there is already much disagreement—production potential, efficiency, relief of institutional constraints on the food system.
- Land use and water use are closely linked to climate, and significant climate change will lead to potentially important changes in their character. Land uses that may be affected include crops, livestock, forests, biomass energy, water quality, and recreation and tourism.
- Climate change will have both positive and negative effects on human activities associated with land use. Whether the net change will be beneficial or damaging is uncertain. The degree to which humans can maximize the benefits and minimize damages will depend upon societal responses.
- Costs of climate change actions can be significantly reduced through effective timing and global trade.
- Sea level rise may result in flooding of coastal zones and inundation of small islands, resulting in displaced populations, loss of animal and plant habitat, and social conflicts over remaining resources. The degree of impact will depend on the timing, nature, and degree of change. Changes may enhance some human activities but degrade others.
- Great uncertainties surround most coastal zone impacts not related to sea level rise, such as those to fisheries and tourism. These impacts include intensification and increased instability of extreme weather events such as cyclones, storm surges, and floods; the spread of diseases with water-borne vectors, such as malaria and cholera; and spoilation of tourist areas.

Institutional constraints may make technically and even financially irreproachable policy measures infeasible.

nations but little loss of life. However, less industrialized and poor nations experience little economic damage but massive loss of life.

Analyses of the present state of land use and water use are hampered by poor data and resultant uncertainties. Since land classification is both a descriptive and a normative activity, no realistic, accurate database on global land use exists. (With remote sensing techniques, data on land cover are better.) Classification problems exemplify a conflict between ecocentric and anthropocentric perspectives; for example, the land-use perspective defines degradation in relation to intended use, not according to biological criteria or net primary production. Water use data are similarly lacking or suspect. Uncertainties include the magnitude of land-use emissions and the sustainability of current land-use practices. The underlying causes of deforestation are also poorly understood, although it is the largest land-use contributor to current atmospheric increases in carbon dioxide.

Two-thirds of the world's people live in coastal zones. The big losers from global climate change are most likely to be small island nations and poor countries with large, densely populated, low-lying coastal areas.

Even without climate change, land use and water use are changing at a rapid pace. Problems that are being created and addressed include overfishing, water pollution, impacts of oil and gas exploration, deforestation, harmful agricultural practices (including overfertilization and inefficient irrigation), tourism (even eco-tourism), and poverty in subsistence economies.

Energy and industry

Energy-use data are much more complete and accurate than those on land use and water use.

Economic analyses of these data, reported in "Energy and industry," show energy demand growing worldwide, but more rapidly in less industrialized than in industrialized nations. Energy intensity has been declining for very long periods of time. The resource base of fossil fuels, the consumption of which is the single largest source of greenhouse-related emissions, places no meaningful constraint on loading carbon into the atmosphere. In particular, the resource base of coal is huge, and 96 percent is within the boundaries of a dozen nations (70 percent within the boundaries of China, Russia, and the United States).

Significant changes in energy use can be expected with or without climate change. However, we have a very poor idea of what the so-called autonomous rate of technological change is.

Significant changes in energy use can be expected with or without climate change. If present trends continue, the world will run out of oil and natural gas at a price it is prepared to pay, and substitutes will have to be found. However, we have a very poor idea of what the so-called autonomous rate of technological change is. New technologies could result in the development of new nonfossil fuels. In any case, population increases and declining fuelwood sources will bring pressure to change fuels in less industrialized countries. The limits of hydropower may be reached, especially considering alternative demands of a growing population for both energy and water resources. Scientists and engineers will continue to develop new energy technologies. The responses of markets, governments, and consumers to changes in the energy system may be influenced significantly by potential or actual climate change. They will almost certainly have an influence on the rate and extent of climate change itself.

 Although there is considerable scope for effective mitigation and adaptation measures, the potential also exists to expend vast resources and have little or nothing to show for it.

The change in the nature and scale of economic activities is both the underlying cause of anthropogenic climate change and perhaps the wellspring of resources with which to mitigate or adapt to climate change. At the same time, the potential exists to expend vast resources in adopting policies of both emissions mitigation and impacts adaptation and have little or nothing to show for it.

Responses to climate change

Social science research tells us a great deal about human activities that give rise to climate change and the societies in which these activities are embedded. This kind of research can identify possible greenhouse gas emissions mitigation actions. It can indicate where adaptations will be necessary. It can also illuminate how institutional and cultural structures and abilities to change will both constrain and open up possibilities to implement climate change policies.

Proposed policy responses to climate change range from, "Do nothing; climate change will be good for us," to Draconian measures that would, at the extremes, require extraordinary frugality or massive geoengineering interventions to control the climate or impacts of climate change. Between these extremes, there is considerable scope for effective, implementable mitigation and adaptation measures to reduce the impacts of climate change. Most of these involve institutional responses. The challenge to social scientists is to understand the complexities arising from the global scope of the problem, cultural and social diversity, the long timescale, and likely discrepancies in impacts.

Reducing emissions

At the present time, the emphasis of almost all policymaking efforts is on reducing greenhouse gas emissions. In fact, in many contexts climate policy or action is equated exclusively with immediate emissions reductions. In some of these discourses it is almost impossible to discuss strategies that emphasize developing technologies with the potential to rapidly displace fossil fuel use at some point in the future.

Research into likely or possible emissions trajectories is confronted with high uncertainties in population, consumption, technology, and social institutions that will change whether or not the climate changes. This has been a major area of research for the kind of energy-economic modeling described in "Energy and industry." The future context will be a world that has changed, with or without climate change. Many paths of development are possible. Indeed, the high and low bounds of population estimates (5 billion to 18 billion in 2100) represent different development paths, not probabilistic confidence intervals. An area of research where the social sciences can make important contributions is in exploring human choices in response to climate change and evaluating the likely results for human societies at global, regional, and local scales.

 The consensus result of cost–benefit analyses is that relatively modest near-term actions are required, although the degree of intervention required to stabilize emissions grows over time. This result depends on several assumptions, the violation of which can change the finding.

The costs of emissions reduction have also been a major line of research in energy-economics modeling and integrated assessment modeling. The costs of reducing emissions, mitigation costs, and alternative pathways and associated cost efficiencies have been extensively studied. The consensus result of studies employing cost–benefit analysis is that relatively modest near-term actions are required, although the degree of intervention required to stabilize emissions grows over time. Equilibrium economic models show costs of efficiently stabilizing fossil fuel carbon emissions under 5 percent of gross domestic product (GDP), with many significantly lower. This result depends on several assumptions, the violation of which can change the finding—for example, the choice of a discount rate and the almost inevitable occurrence of surprises. Although the value of the discount rate is extremely important in determining the optimal degree of emissions mitigation, the problem of determining a single correct discount rate is fundamentally unresolvable. Furthermore, economic tools remain crude for handling surprises.

Stabilizing concentrations

Policymakers have focused on reducing emissions, but stabilizing the concentration of greenhouse gases at the equivalent of 500 ppmv of carbon dioxide may be less expensive than stabilizing emissions that lead to concentrations in excess of 500 ppmv after the year 2100. Substituting among greenhouse gases can significantly reduce the cost of meeting any emissions mitigation goal, although the appropriate method for calculating global warming potential (GWP) coefficients for different greenhouse-related gases continues to remain unsettled.

Cost-effective mitigation paths are generally characterized by emissions that grow in the early years, peak, and then decline in later years. Delaying emissions mitigation can reduce costs of achieving a target by:

- taking advantage of the carbon-cycle emissions bonus (i.e., carbon released earlier in a given time period would have a smaller concentration than carbon released later in the time period)
- gaining from technological change that can be reasonably anticipated to provide more efficient technologies over time
- avoiding premature retirement and inappropriate conversion of capital stocks
- taking advantage of the time-cost discounting (i.e., the further in the future a given economic burden lies, the smaller the resources that must be set aside today to undertake it).

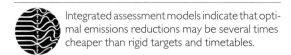

Integrated assessment models indicate that optimal emissions reductions may be several times cheaper than rigid targets and timetables.

However, these potential advantages would come at the price of somewhat higher intermediate-term carbon dioxide concentrations than may be unacceptable to activist constituencies who are concerned that the anticipated long-term benefits may not be realized.

Various alternative emissions paths can satisfy the goal of the FCCC for any carbon dioxide concentration ceiling chosen. Introducing flexibility about when emissions reductions are achieved can allow participants in an international agreement to lower costs by shifting emissions mitigation in time to accommodate special circumstances. Integrated assessment models indicate that such optimal emissions reductions may be several times cheaper than rigid targets and timetables.

Similarly, the degree of flexibility about where emissions are mitigated significantly affects the cost of achieving any emissions mitigation goal. In principle, this observation would lend support to allowing emissions trading and concentrating early actions in less industrialized countries where the emissions reduction potential per dollar spent would seem to be greatest. But strong voices express ethical objections to the industrialized nations failing to take the lead in emissions reductions at home. Furthermore, the degree to which less industrialized nations can achieve low-cost mitigation is uncertain and greatly affects the magnitude of calculated savings.

Emissions reduction strategies are dominated by the energy sector. In the long run, the assumptions analysts make about substitutes for oil and gas determine the cost of controlling emissions in their analyses. If conventional oil and gas resources are significantly more (or less) abundant than currently thought, the cost of mitigation could significantly increase (or decrease). Along with resource abundance issues, energy technology developments will have a major impact on the cost of emissions mitigation. Policymakers can influence energy infrastructure development through direct investments in research and development.

No-regrets emissions mitigation opportunities in land-use change will probably be limited, although some low-cost opportunities such as afforestation (especially if used as a transition to biomass energy) may exist. However, biodiversity may be significantly affected by emission mitigation measures that encourage large-scale biomass energy crops. These may lead to increased land-use change emissions as the extent of intensively managed lands expands to provide both agriculture and energy to a fossil fuel-constrained world.

No nation, no matter how large or important, can stabilize global emissions independently.

Adherence to different equity positions leads to different economic consequences. An allocation of emissions rights on the basis of historical emissions leads to a transfer of wealth from less industrialized nations to more industrialized nations and a greater cost burden on the former. The reverse is true when emissions are allocated on the basis of equal per capita adult populations (although such transfers may not sufficiently compensate some nations for participating in an emissions reduction protocol). Allocating emissions rights on the basis of income or GDP results in smaller transfers of wealth than either of the above bases.

Whatever route toward stabilization is chosen, clearly no nation, no matter how large or important, can stabilize global emissions independently. Even the countries of the OECD, which accept the heaviest burden of initial responsibility as signatories of the FCCC, could not independently stabilize the atmosphere. Although all nations need not participate, a significant share of emissions must be controlled by participants in any protocol to mitigate emissions. In addition, any agreement to control fossil fuel carbon emissions, no matter how skillfully crafted, will require a process of constant revision in the terms of participation because the economic needs of its participants will be evolving.

Adaptation

The need for adaptation to climate change impacts is inevitable because of the existing commitment that humanity has already made to climate change through past emissions and future emissions that are inevitable, even under the most Draconian emissions reduction targets possible. To stabilize atmospheric concentrations of carbon dioxide overnight, even at present levels, would require emissions reductions roughly equivalent to everyone outside of North America ceasing entirely to emit by tomorrow morning. Hence, adaptation is, at the very least, an essential complement to emissions reductions. Why then does adaptation receive so little attention in international negotiations and national climate change policy programs? It seems that the climate change policy community refrains from serious discussions of adaptation for fear that discussion of the possibility of adaptation will attenuate the pressure to reduce emissions, even though any reduction target that is seriously under discussion in international arenas will still leave significant room for climate impacts to occur.

The need for adaptation to climate change impacts is inevitable.

Adaptation potential varies significantly across natural and human systems and depends crucially on financial resources, natural resource endowments, and social relationships—that is to say on access to financial, natural, and social capital. Although financial capital is widely understood and interest in defining and valuing natural capital is receiving more attention, social capital is poorly understood and largely ignored by policymakers. This situation is particularly unfortunate for economically poorer countries, because social capital is the only one of the three forms of capital to increase, rather than dissipate, with use. It would seem to be an essential factor in any efforts to reduce the vulnerability of those countries to climate impacts. Resource endowments and financial capital can be traded off against each other, perhaps more easily than social capital. A wealthy country that is also endowed with appropriate natural resources, such as the United States, has a strong potential to adapt to climate impacts on human populations and managed ecosystems. Americans have the capability, at a price, to install more air conditioning, adjust crop varieties and cropping practices, and buy food from elsewhere if US production falls. The United States has both the wealth and the materials to build sea walls if it chooses to protect its coastal zones from intrusion by the seas. In marked contrast, Bangladesh lacks even wood or stone to build sea defenses, but imports rubble from other countries for building projects. Certainly, Bangladesh does not have access to the capital that would be required to protect its population from sea level rise or storms and, even if it did, it has more pressing development priorities. Until we understand the role and dynamics of social capital better, it appears that adaptation is essentially an option for the wealthy. On the other hand, human populations such as those of Bangladesh seem to be able to restore business-as-usual much more quickly and readily than those of industrialized nations. The industrialized world may have much to learn from the less industrialized nations about the issue of resilience.

Until we understand the role and dynamics of social capital better, it appears that adaptation is essentially an option for the wealthy.

As "Reasoning by analogy" shows, in some cases, adaptation would result in social, cultural, and economic upheaval and departure from familiar, perhaps ancestral homelands. For some low-lying island nations, no credible program of sea-wall construction would preserve them from sea and storms. Such large-scale engineering programs would in any case irreparably damage the way of life that holds the people of low-lying island communities together. If climate impacts become severe, some will not be able to adapt. Although this is unfortunate, it is by no means a new or unique situation. Coastal civilizations have been inundated by the ocean or displaced by volcanoes since classical times and before. Recent examples of islands becoming uninhabitable include Tristan da Cuhna and Montserrat. These examples of displacement of whole societies remind us that it can happen and suggest that at least some attention should be paid now to the issue of how best to deal with the situation should it arise. Such precautions could include research into how to preserve the social capital of affected populations, and establishment of international funds that could be invested against the day when such impacts occur.

Beneficial policies for adaptation to climate change may include opportunities for reducing other kinds of environmental and socioeconomic risks. For example, increasing the resistance of crops and people to heat and drought or securing the sustainable stewardship of freshwater supplies for home and agricultural use will bring indisputable benefits even in the absence of climate change. For adaptation policies, there is much less room for skepticism about the existence of no-regrets investments in research and policy measures. Various adaptation options can be pursued at relatively low cost compared to emissions reductions, especially those that involve correcting existing economic inefficiencies. This is an important role for markets. Government also has an important role in promoting effective research and development for adaptation options, in lowering domestic barriers to cost-effective adaptive measures, and in promoting low-cost international cooperation. Civil society and communities will also have an important role to play in developing and contributing social capital to provide the underpinnings of mutual support and capability for the social, political, and economic strategy switching that will be necessary for any successful adaptation policy strategy.

How do governments establish where climate change stands in relation to other political priorities?

As the authors of "Institutions for political action" argue, global climate change, a long-term issue with uncertain benefits, is constantly liable to be displaced from policymakers' attention by more immediate issues such as economic problems or national security questions. In that sense, climate change policy has a relatively weak constituency.

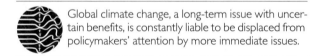

Global climate change, a long-term issue with uncertain benefits, is constantly liable to be displaced from policymakers' attention by more immediate issues.

On the other hand, the threat of climate change can be a useful political stick for governments to wave while pursuing other agendas. For example, in the United Kingdom, Margaret Thatcher's environmentalist epiphany in 1989 can be viewed in terms of her determination to eliminate once and for all the political threat to Conservative Party governments posed by the powerful National Union of Mineworkers. Similarly, the German government took up the climate change issue at the same time as it began a major push to restructure German industry.

Although the nation state remains the principal locus of political action, its claims to unique legitimacy and effectiveness must be tempered by the

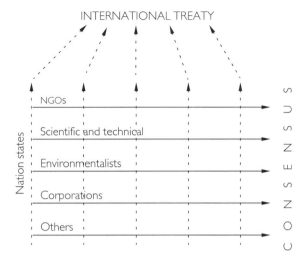

Figure 3.1 A polycentric model of international decisionmaking (Rayner 1991).

institutional innovations of the global society. Political influence and real power is diffusing to international and domestic policy networks in which governments and their agencies interact directly with social movements, firms, and communities. "Thus, state power remains extremely strategic, but it is no longer the only game in town" (Pieterse 1995).

Increasingly, the once-orderly picture of the relationships among states and governance within states is giving way to a more turbulent, even chaotic, pattern of crisscrossing solidarities in which communities of interest and identity form multiple networks horizontally across national boundaries, vertically within nested jurisdictions of societal sectors, and diagonally across borders and sectors simultaneously (Fig. 3.1). "Institutions for political action" describes how the framework of the realist school in international relations, based on the idea of anarchy among nations whose primary concern is their own sovereignty, falls short of providing an adequate understanding of global environmental politics, but alternative models to understand international relationships may not have caught up to help us understand and work within the current international setting.

Material growth remains a legitimate policy of every nation, and entrenched patterns of interests and representation sustain a bias in favor of activities that lead to increasing greenhouse-related emissions in the foreseeable future. These patterns of interest are reinforced not only by the nation state but by other important players: bureaucracies, citizen groups, and businesses. Domestically, policy networks that link state agencies and nongovernmental actors provide opportunities for the development of policy. They are relatively open, exchange information relatively freely, and can informally enforce consensus or block action. They shift according to changes in political party, problem analysis, technology, external relationships, key personalities entering and leaving, and internal restructuring.

 Although the nation state remains the principal locus of political action, political influence and real power is diffusing to international and domestic policy networks in which governments and their agencies interact directly with social movements, firms, and communities.

Policy networks provide one model of institutional change; the notion of standard operating procedures offers another. Organizations process new problems through a template of procedures, rather than fully considering multiple alternatives. Although this reduces uncertainty and complexity in the policymaking process, it also limits the range of possible policy, perhaps (or probably) excluding better approaches than the one adopted. However, creating interdepartmental committees and environmental policy units have counteracted this tendency by introducing changes and expansions in organizational templates, encouraging institutional change and innovation.

How are policy instruments chosen?

Locating global climate change issues in a set of issues—including pollution, environmental degradation, food production, poverty, equity, and governance—may result in integrated policies to address multiple issues in ways that are understandable and implementable at local, regional, and global levels. Social science research provides frameworks for designing such policies, taking into account uncertainties and diverse viewpoints (Box 3.2). Diverse and contradictory viewpoints mean that agreements need to include multiple pathways to the agreed-upon goals.

"Institutions for political action" describes the policy instruments available to address mitigation and adaptation issues. These instruments include taxes, marketable allowances, command-and-control technology-based approaches, and dissemination of information. Differences in the performance among policy instruments seem to be better explained by variations in the institutional circumstances under which they are employed than by any inherent characteristics of the instruments themselves.

Any policymaking process must consider what can be expected to occur at the international and national levels. For example, the track record of the

Box 3.2   Elements of an effective climate change policy

The research literature reviewed in *Human choice and climate change* provides some insights into elements of effective climate change policy:

- Effective actions designed to mitigate or respond opportunistically or adaptively to climate change are likely to be those that are most fully integrated into more general policy strategies for economic and social development. The more that climate change issues are routinized as part of the planning perspective at the appropriate level of implementation (e.g., the firm or community), the more likely they are to achieve desired goals. Climate change policies unconnected to other issues will be hard to implement.
- The real business of responding to climate concerns may well be through smaller, often less formal, agreements among states, states and firms, firms and nongovernmental organizations or communities, and so forth.
- Policymakers should more and more work toward a continuous framework of interactive negotiation in which policy explicitly becomes the formalization of actions being undertaken by participating parties.
- The most likely zone of effective implementation is at the regional and local levels, subject to national commitments through broad international agreements. In federal constitutions, the regional focus is important, although local action at a city level will tend to be more influential.
- Programs for implementation should exploit political, economic, and cultural diversity. Policymakers need to pay more explicit attention to why different constituencies prefer different instruments and diversify implementation packages. And they should supplement policy instruments by harnessing indigenous traditional mechanisms of social regulation.
- Policymakers and scientists should work towards integrating science and social goals; this would increase the credibility of ruling institutions and join the methods and goals of scientific inquiry with people's felt needs and with lay systems of acquiring, testing, and acting upon knowledge.
- Policy should include a concept of fairness that acknowledges diversity across more than distributional outcome alone. Considerations should include fair allocations of mitigation and adaptation costs, the allocation of wealth that would allow fair international bargaining, and the fair allocation of greenhouse-related gases in both the short and long term.
- For new technologies, strategic niche management has the advantage over traditional supply and demand policies of promoting technical change in directions that offer both short-term and long-term benefits.
- In crafting policy for technological research and development, policymakers should invest in activities that will change the "rules of the game," for example, by increasing the number of players, empowering certain voices, promoting information exchange and learning, stimulating cooperation, and in general facilitating change. Policymakers should think of a heuristic approach that identifies points of attachment to evolving sociotechnical landscapes.
- Alternative policy strategies will need to be cast in the context of expanding international market sectors.

The overall challenge is to create the right balance between simplicity and complexity, aggregation and disaggregation, the needs of present populations and needs of future generations, stochastic and deterministic behavior, quantitative and qualitative linkages, social and natural sciences, and exogenous and endogenous processes. The use of multiple tools and varying assumptions help to test the validity of results and conclusions to the policymaking context.

At global and national levels, a "one-size-fits-all" approach to policy instruments will fail.

international community in monitoring and ensuring compliance with environmental agreements reflects its poor performance in policing international agreements and treaties. Domestically, an environmental treaty may take a shorter amount of time to be ratified if the country's quality of life is high. Setting aside the question of ratification, we cannot expect climate change policies to be effective where institutional infrastructures are inadequate.

Different kinds of instruments seem to be inherently attractive to different constituencies that exercise very different levels of political and economic power within different countries (Fig. 3.2). Private sector institutions favor instruments that leave discretion with firms. Government agencies favor instruments that leave discretion to regulators. Environmental groups favor arrangements that do not permit discretion at all for fear of it being abused by regulatory agencies.

The choice of policy instruments seems to be subject to fashions. In environmental matters, the first wave of policy instruments was regulatory. This gave way to instruments employing fiscal incentives, arguably more effective and less costly to monitor. In the past few years, new instruments have emphasized

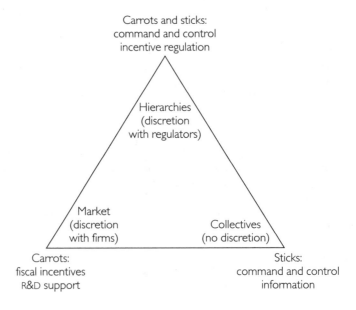

Figure 3.2 A policy space for implementation instruments (Rayner 1991).

100

voluntary aspects, for example, the Joint Implementation initiative and US proposed actions under the President's Climate Change Action Plan.

At global and national levels, a "one-size-fits-all" approach to policy instruments will fail; any one instrument will not account for the diverse social arrangements, knowledge, and knowledge flows at local and regional levels. Policies at higher levels must provide multiple pathways to meet goals and provisions for using local knowledge.

Why and how did the international community choose to address climate change?

Social scientists study the emergence of policy issues, such as the path by which a hitherto sparsely funded set of basic Earth systems sciences, such as atmospheric chemistry and climatology, managed to emerge from obscurity to command research resources on the scale of the IPCC or the annual US global change research budget of about $1.5 billion. According to the knowledge-based approach to agenda setting, there is little to be explained. It is a the result of policymakers' sensitivities being heightened by scientific information concerning potentially very large stakes and containing significant uncertainties that must be reduced by research. The knowledge-based approach also focuses on the issue of saliency, pointing out that the explosion of interest in the United States coincided with the continent-wide drought of 1988.

However, closer scrutiny renders this account unsatisfying. There were major drought events throughout the course of the past century. At the same time, the essential scientific information about the greenhouse effect was available for 92 years prior to the 1988 drought. Arrhenius, writing in the *London, Edinburgh, and Dublin Philosophical Magazine* of April 1896 identified the greenhouse effect and even calculated the expected degrees of warming at various latitudes that he expected in the doubled carbon dioxide scenario that is used as the benchmark by contemporary climate modelers. Without even a pocket calculator, Arrhenius arrived at figures only a couple of degrees higher than today's scientists have been able to achieve with the latest supercomputers. In recent decades, we have obtained direct measurements of rapidly rising concentrations of carbon dioxide in the atmosphere, as well as ice-core records indicating that these increases are part of a trend dating from the industrial revolution. There have been slight increases in global average temperatures over the course of the century. These are legitimate causes for concern, but seem hardly the stuff to grab headlines for more than a few days, let alone stimulate a major scientific effort and political initiative to make fundamental changes in global energy use and the world's economy.

In contrast with the knowledge-based approach, which locates the ultimate cause for concern in nature, a political cultural account focuses on factors such as:

- the decline of scientific and technological optimism since the 1950s
- a widespread retreat from the view widely held in the first half of the century that both nature and society could be reduced to complete systematic descriptions that would ensure human control over the world
- the use of external threats (whether from nature, alien cultures, or subversive ideologies) as an instrument of social cohesion and control
- the perennial tension in human society, highlighted by the end of the Cold War, between advocates of independence and of interdependence in human organization.

From the political–cultural standpoint, climate change and other phenomena gathered under the rubric of global environmental change are convenient hypotheses available to be taken up as political cudgels in the struggle between market-oriented worldview stressing individuality and independence and the rival view of mutual responsibility and interdependence. Indeed, Wildavsky, a social scientist, in his introduction to skeptical climatologist Balling's book *The heated debate* (1992), makes just such an argument. However, the political–cultural account of issue emergence cannot be taken, as Wildavsky takes it, to resolve scientific uncertainty in favor of dismissing concern about global climate change.

Irrespective of the specific uncertainties involved in the climate debate, ecological and socioeconomic interdependence is clearly a reality in a world where industrial development and land-use change are occurring at an unprecedented scale and pace. The social science account of the emergence of climate as a public policy issue offers a bridge between the issues of the global environment and of global governance.

How do societies select technologies that cause, mitigate, or assist adaptation to climate change?

Technological developments over the past 300 years have enabled humans to conduct economic activities on a scale sufficient both to support vast improvements in human conditions and to contribute to changes in the atmosphere leading toward global climatic changes. Researchers have explored the potential for technology developments that may mitigate climate change and the cost-efficiency implications of various scenarios for new technology implementation. Social scientists have also studied how technological development

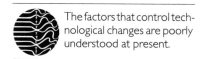

The factors that control technological changes are poorly understood at present.

proceeds, from attempts to provide incentives for certain types of innovation to the process of technology adoption and diffusion.

Our ideas about the role of technology depend first upon our notions of what technology is. Technology is, of course, more than tools. "Technological change" describes how social scientists have expanded its meaning to encompass artifacts, human capital, institutional arrangements, and social structures. Technologies evolve out a social context; their success is linked in some way to structural problems or even crises of that context. But technologies, as they succeed, can grow to the point at which they set the context into which newer technologies must evolve. An established technology is one that has become an integral part of the sociotechnical landscape, establishing the terms of competition for other technologies. For example, all new technologies for generating electricity must compete with existing, economically viable technologies powered by fossil fuels.

The factors that control technological changes are poorly understood at present. Technology is neither a cannonball (coming from somewhere outside society and having an impact) nor an endless reservoir (upon which society can draw to fix its problems). Using these kinds of common metaphors explicitly or implicitly may result in policies that do more harm than good, because they are not informed by the complex linkages among tools, systems, and societies.

Directing technology developments or implementation is difficult at best. The goals are usually not particularly clear, nor are the strategies sure-fire. Command and control works only in very special circumstances, usually with unintended and unanticipated consequences. The processes of technology development and diffusion can be fostered if a niche or niches provide a protected environment for growth. If the technology has a specialized application or appeal for a certain type of consumer, it can be developed as it is applied, improving its competitiveness outside the niche. For example, the early automobile found a market among rural doctors, for whom the benefits outweighed the inconveniences. Within this niche market, automobiles were improved enough to find wider markets, as recounted in "Technological change."

The research demonstrates that technology is neither a simple nor a sure solution to energy use or emissions problems. Rather, social scientists understand technology as sociotechnical configurations that are partially embedded in institutional structures. New technologies can probably be stimulated only indirectly.

How can research on social choice be useful to the global climate change debate?

Choice is a theme that runs up and down the scale, from individual consumption choices to global climate change treaties among states. At any scale, the choices made by people, groups of people, and institutions have determined what greenhouse gases have been emitted to the atmosphere; these choices will determine what, if anything, will be done to mitigate or adapt to climate change. If researchers and policymakers do not seek to understand how choices are made and how choices at one scale become operative at other scales, the success of their policies will be only a matter of luck.

An individual is multidimensional, that is, he or she is not just a consumer, making marketplace decisions based on cost. Membership of various social groups and networks influences the choices an individual makes. Several chapters, including "Needs and wants," "Cultural discourses," "Institutions for political action," and "Decision analysis" emphasize that the values of these groups and networks and the individual manifestations of these values are important. How does an individual internalize the institutional pressures of the groups or networks that he or she belongs to? This process is neither random nor unpredictable; patterns emerge both in institutional values and in people's responses to them. The research problem is then to analyze how people reconcile or accommodate competing social preferences for action, not how to aggregate individual preferences into a collective preference. Stated this way, the research problem is scale independent, that is, collective choice processes can be analyzed at household, community, market, regional, national, and international levels.

Social science research demonstrates that the process through which choices articulate across scales is not a linear mechanism that consistently produces the most rational alternative at the next-highest scale. Rather, it is a social as well as a knowledge process that requires a high level of trust and agreement (including standardization of methods and results) to gain recognition at another scale. Moreover, like and Escher image (Fig. 3.3), the direction of the process is not always clear. In the process, some ideas and knowledge will be ignored or discarded, and these may form the basis of a backlash movement.

Research that describes choice processes is important; equally important is research that describes processes by which individuals can be persuaded to conform with new normative requirements of corporations and governments, as implemented by the decisionmakers who are their officials. Once an agreement is reached—for example, by the Conference of the Parties of the FCCC—how can that agreement be implemented "on the ground," where choices are made that directly affect the rate and extent of greenhouse gas emissions?

Figure 3.3 *Relativity*, by M. C. Escher (lithograph, 1953), illustrating the nonlinear, complex, and uncertain nature of the social processes that link knowledge and actions across various scales.

These issues of choice involve fundamental social science research that is directly relevant to global climate change. Our models of rationality tell only part of the story and give only a partial and distorted picture of how real-world choices are made. Market-based models that include the undifferentiated rational consumer work well at the macro scale and with all its assumptions satisfied. However, decisionmakers need to complement or supplement such models with those that allow for uncertainty and diversity.

The importance of climate change

Barring changes such as would transform the habitability of the world, climate change is probably not the deciding factor in whether human society in the aggregate prospers, maintains itself, or declines. More important factors are the resilience of human institutions (i.e., human abilities to adapt and to cooperate). However, changes in regional patterns of habitability would exacerbate existing problems and cause major damage to poor populations in environmentally fragile areas. Although aggregated global effects may be negligible, regional effects may be severe, including violent storms, inundation caused by sea level rise, and formerly fertile land becoming unsuitable for agriculture.

 Barring changes such as would transform the habitability of the world, climate change is probably not the deciding factor in whether human society in the aggregate prospers.

Global climate change will be inexorable, but also incremental, and will be set against a social, political, and economic background that is far different from the present. In fact, social and political structures and processes will probably change faster than the IPCC projects for climate. This difference in rates of change may lead policymakers to delay taking action to mitigate or adapt to climate change until disaster overtakes them. However, the same difference also has the potential to allow societies to stay ahead of climate change, that is, to build in the capability to forecast and respond effectively to many Earth systems changes resulting from climate change.

Whether or not humanity realizes the potential to get ahead and stay ahead of climate change depends on what happens on the ground, at the micro levels of consumption and voting behavior. Researchers and policymakers should not become absorbed by potential global-level impacts, but rather they should focus on regional issues and potential problems. Future technological and economic developments might help mitigate the effects of changing climate. On the whole, people living in the future will probably be wealthier than our contemporaries and will be better buffered from the shocks that weather and climate produce. But the number of people to be supported will be greater, poor populations may be larger, and environmentally fragile areas will likely be subject to the most stress, potentially putting more people at risk.

Diversity, complexity, and uncertainty will frustrate the search for top-down global policymaking and implementation. Social science research in all disciplines indicates that policymakers should attempt to reach agreement on high-level environmental and associated social goals, then look for local and regional opportunities to use policy in various ways appropriate to the institutional

On the whole, people living in the future will probably be wealthier than our contemporaries and will be better buffered from the shocks that weather and climate produce. But the number of people to be supported will be greater, poor populations may be larger, and environmentally fragile areas will likely be subject to the most stress, potentially putting more people at risk.

arrangements, cultural values, economic and political conditions, and environmental changes.

References

Arrhenius, S. 1896. On the influence of carbonic acid in the air upon the temperature of the ground. *London, Edinburgh, and Dublin Philosophical Magazine and Journal of Science*, S5 **41**(251), 237–76.

Balling Jr, R. C. 1992. *The heated debate: greenhouse predictions versus climate reality*. San Francisco: Pacific Research Institute for Public Policy.

Brooks, H. 1976. The federal government and the autonomy of scholarship. In *Controversies and decisions: the social sciences and public policy*, C. Frankel (ed.). New York: Russell Sage Foundation.

Bruce, J. P., H. Lee, E. F. Haites (eds) 1996. *Climate change 1995: economic and social dimensions of climate change*. Cambridge: Cambridge University Press.

Kempton, W. 1991. Lay perspectives on global climate change. *Global Environmental Change: Human and Policy Dimensions* **1**(3), 183–208.

Kempton, W., J. S. Boster, J. A. Hartley 1995. *Environmental values in American culture*. Boston: MIT Press.

Kunreuther, H., R. Ginsberg, L. Miller, P. Sagi, P. Slovic, B. Borkan, N. Katz 1978. *Disaster insurance protection: public policy lessons*. New York: John Wiley.

Pearce, D. W., W. R. Cline, A. N. Achanta, S. Fankhauser, R. K. Pachauri, R. S. J. Tol, P. Vellinga 1996. The social costs of climate change: greenhouse damage and the benefits of control. In *Climate change 1995: economic and social dimensions of climate change*, J. P. Bruce, H. Lee, E. G. Haites (eds). Cambridge: Cambridge University Press.

Pieterse, J. N. 1995. Globalization as hybridization. In *Global modernities*, M. Featherstone, S. Lash, R. Robertson (eds). London: Sage.

Watson, R. T., M. C. Zinyowera, R. H. Moss (eds) 1996. *Climate change 1995: impacts, adaptations and mitigation*. Cambridge: Cambridge University Press.

CHAPTER 4

Ten suggestions for policymakers

Steve Rayner & Elizabeth L. Malone

If public and private decisionmakers find any merit in the four volumes of *Human choice and climate change*, what might they do differently? What have we learned from a wide-ranging look at the social sciences and the issue of human choice and climate change that illuminates the evaluation of policy goals, implementation strategies, and choices about paths forward? At present, proposed policies are heavily focused on the development and implementation of intergovernmental agreements on immediate emissions reductions. In the spirit of cognitive and analytic pluralism that has guided the our project, we look beyond the present policy priorities to see if there are adjustments, or even wholesale changes, to the present course that could be made on the basis of a social science perspective. To this end we offer ten suggestions to complement and challenge existing approaches to public and private sector decisionmaking:

- **View the issue of climate change holistically, not just as the problem of emissions reductions.**
- **Recognize that, for climate policymaking, institutional limits to global sustainability are at least as important as environmental limits.**
- **Prepare for the likelihood that social, economic, and technological change will be more rapid and have greater direct impacts on human populations than climate change.**
- **Recognize the limits of rational planning.**
- **Employ the full range of analytic perspectives and decision aids from the natural and social sciences and the humanities in climate change policymaking.**
- **Design policy instruments for real world conditions rather than try to make the world conform to a particular policy model.**
- **Incorporate climate change concerns into other more immediate issues, such as employment, defense, economic development, and public health.**
- **Take a regional and local approach to climate policymaking and implementation.**
- **Direct resources into identifying vulnerability and promoting resilience, especially where the impacts will be largest.**
- **Use a pluralistic approach to decisionmaking.**

We begin with the current focus of climate change policy research and practice on emissions reductions.

View the issue of climate change holistically,
not just as the problem of emissions reductions

A re-examination of the present policy path seems particularly pertinent at the time *Human choice and climate change* is going to press. The overwhelming priority placed on emissions reduction since emissions reduction goals of 20 percent by 2005 were proposed at the 1988 Toronto Conference on Climate Change has almost entirely displaced attention to the evaluation and development of adaptive policy responses (and entirely eliminated consideration of any possibilities of geoengineering responses). Since the Toronto conference the additional radiative forcing effect of greenhouse-related gases on the planet's surface has risen by a little more than half a watt per m^2, about one-fifth of the total increase in the forcing effect from the beginning of the Industrial Revolution up to 1990. Concentrations of carbon dioxide have risen about five times the historical average for the decades between the onset of the Industrial Revolution and 1988. Emissions have fallen substantially in some countries, but only because of economic collapse that has added to the sum of human misery. Of the economically healthy countries that have set themselves voluntary emissions reduction targets of returning to 1990 emission levels, only Britain and Germany have succeeded, but for reasons unconnected to climate change; a Conservative British government having broken the political power of the National Union of Mineworkers by switching from coal to nuclear electricity generation and the so-called dash for gas, and Germany by reaping the unintended consequences of the restructuring of the economy of the former German Democratic Republic.

An emissions limitation strategy has the distinct advantage that it is reasonably easy to get one's arms around conceptually. The justification of such measures is that they represent at least a start down the right road. However, in practice, the 20 percent level of emissions reductions currently under discussion for the industrialized countries seems to have little, if any, basis in the levels actually required for stabilization of atmospheric concentrations of greenhouse-related gases. The target seems to be entirely a negotiating construct based on the participants' assessment of what is achievable politically.

The targets and timetables approach has also proven to be extremely divisive in the United States, which is presently the largest total and per capita emitter. Such division is likely to endure so long as people with a broad cross-section of worldviews and economic interests lack compelling evidence that emissions reductions would be cost effective. There is also a likelihood that emissions reductions at levels that fail to provide the environmental benefits sought will gives rise to a backlash against such policies. Such a backlash could be exacerbated in countries that make economic sacrifices to meet targets if other countries appear to be making less effort or improving their competitiveness thereby.

The direct approach to mitigation through targets and timetables sidesteps other processing issues of human welfare. Social science research indicates that the people who are most likely to suffer serious impacts from climate change are future generations of poor people living in vulnerable parts of the tropics. Is incurring greenhouse gas mitigation costs necessarily the best or even the most equitable way to help future victims if it leaves their parents and grandparents enmeshed in the quagmire of poverty and resource degradation? Why do we seem to be so deeply concerned about future generations of poor people in developing countries while we seem so indifferent to those who are alive today? Might not decisive global action to tackle destitution and resource impoverishment be a more effective allocation of global resources than forcibly accelerating the demise of fossil fuels? In the present negotiating environment, such questions cannot even be posed because of the hegemonic grip that the emissions reduction strategy has on the policy discourse.

The voices most loudly demanding prompt action on climate change almost invariably equate action with immediate emissions reductions on the part of industrialized countries. Other components of a response strategy, such as a focus on developing nonfossil energy technologies to displace fossil fuels wherever new generating capacity is added, have often been hastily dismissed as stalling tactics. Denunciation has been swift for analysts who have dared even to question the cost-effectiveness of the proposed timing of reductions in defiance of the oft-repeated, but unproven assertion that reductions should be made as early as possible because the costs of mitigation will rise over time. But surely, emissions reductions, especially in any particular pattern, are not an end but a means? From a social perspective—which may differ from an ecocentric one—the end must lie in securing and improving the overall quality of human life.

The thirst for a simple answer to a simple problem may represent a significant obstacle to humanity's ability to deal with the complex realities of climate change, albeit perhaps in a less directed, even less rational, way. At the very least, the debate about climate policy must be broadened beyond the issue of mitigation by emissions reductions, even if only because our past emissions of greenhouse gases and the timescale for any plausible emissions reduction program leaves the planet with an unavoidable commitment to some appreciable degree of climate change impact. Humanity can no longer indulge those who refuse to discuss adaptation with the same fervor that the religious right refuses to countenance sex education, out of fear that it will only encourage dangerous experimentation. For better or worse, we are already pregnant.

To be sure, we are not arguing that emissions should not be reduced. Obviously, present trends, continued indefinitely, will inflict consequential damage on the Earth's ecosystems and economies. But, whatever emissions reductions goals are established, the findings of "Energy and industry" suggest that they should be based on the best available scientific information as well as on assumptions about what is politically tolerable. They should also be established in such a way as to allow countries the maximum flexibility in how, where, and when they pursue reductions, and finally, they should be subject to continuous reassessment in the light of new information.

It is even worth questioning whether targets and timetables are the best way to achieve emissions reductions at all. Essentially they represent the end-of-pipe approach to pollution at the global scale. This approach is increasingly recognized as obsolete for environmental management at local and national levels. Why then does it remain the favored tool for global environmental governance? At the global level, policymakers have the opportunity to leapfrog the end-of-pipe phase.

Accumulating some experience with adaptation could provide a complementary, even perhaps an alternative, model for pursuing emissions reductions. In contrast to governments setting national targets for top-down implementation, there may be some merit in exploring ways in which people—in homes, factories, and fields, and on the roads—can be empowered institutionally and technologically to change the way they do their business in accordance with their individual self-interest and collective values and at the same time contribute to substantial emission reductions without formal targets and timetables.

In other words, policymakers should at least ask whether there is anything to be learned from adaptation that would assist the process of actual emissions reductions (as distinct from the formal process of agreeing national targets). The perspectives on social capital and self-organizing systems discussed in *Human choice and climate change* suggest that there might be. This learning might take the form of developing social and technological strategies focused on institutional arrangements whose routine operations would encourage the production of environmental goods rather than bads. In other words, decisionmakers should encourage the generation of social capital and accompanying capabilities to exercise community responsibility and the dematerialization of industrial processes, without aiming at a particular goal or explicit target for emissions reductions.

Approaching the climate issue from the other end, from that of assessing human vulnerability and social adaptation, may be far less amenable to concerted rational action by national governments than implementing emissions reduction targets. But, it also may be more directly relevant to stakeholders. Adaptation is by nature a variegated response. An adaptation measure designed to protect a coastal community from sea-level rise may have no feature or characteristic in common with measures designed to stem desertification.

113

That is to say, adaptation is a bottom-up strategy that starts with changes and pressures experienced in people's daily lives. This is in marked contrast with the top-down characteristic of national targets for emissions reductions. The connections between emissions targets and people's everyday behavior and responsibilities seem less direct, even abstract. Designing adaptation strategies may be more sensitive to the real tradeoffs made by real people in a way that top-down emissions reduction strategies may not be.

An almost exclusive emphasis on emissions reductions simplifies and bounds climate change as a distinct problem. In so doing it domesticates a large, complex, and unruly set of life's circumstances as being capable of solution through applying of rational analysis, goal setting, and policy implementation by technocratic elites. Questioning the policy emphasis on emissions not only calls into question whether the emphasis is the right one, but whether such an exclusively rational technocratic approach to policymaking is appropriate at all.

Recognize that institutional limits to global sustainability are at least as important for climate policymaking as environmental limits

The technocratic worldview sees nature as presenting decisionmakers with hard constraints, whereas social arrangements are somehow soft and malleable through public information, regulation, price adjustments, or the exercise of a somewhat elusive force referred to as political will. *Human choice and climate change* suggests that institutional arrangements are much harder to change than the technocratic world view suggests. They may also be more important to human welfare than natural resources or events.

Among geophysical agents, weather events are by far the most lethal to humankind worldwide. Together floods, hurricanes, and droughts account for 75 percent of the world's natural disasters. Only earthquakes exact a comparable toll. "Reasoning by analogy" puts such hazards in perspective by noting that losses of life during the twentieth century have been overwhelmingly the result of war, civil strife, and famine —the latter sometimes related to but not simply caused by drought—rather than geophysical events.

The elements that are omitted when climate impacts are treated as wholly climatic are those characteristics of societies, individuals, groups, places, systems, and activities that cause them to lose or gain to differing degrees from particular climate anomalies. Knowing the physical attributes of a climatic variation or change is never adequate for understanding or predicting its consequences for human society. Such is the case for climate hazards; it may reasonably be assumed by analogy to be the case for global climate change. The intense concentration of research effort to date on projecting the physical attributes of a climate change thus scants an equally essential task—that of clarifying what those attributes mean and for whom.

Tackling emissions is recognized as attacking the proximate cause. Analysts and policymakers identify three underlying causes: overpopulation, over-consumption, and inappropriate technology choice attributable to poor pricing and allocation of property rights. Without necessarily buying into the $I=PAT$ equation criticized in "Population and health," policymakers have generally centered discussions around these three elements, which dominate the search for solutions.

Population control won't provide the answer to climate change. Although major factors in fertility reduction are known, these play out differently in different cultures, so that success or failure of population control programs cannot be predicted. Where such programs are effective, they may result in age distributions so skewed as to raise other societal problems (e.g., the consequences of the one-child policy in China). Even if family planning becomes more widely practiced, it is likely to contribute to better spacing of children and better child health than to a drastic change in projected population rates. In any case, projections show population growth set to level off at a globally supportable level, although certainly not one that would be supportable at the current per capita emissions rate of the industrialized world. The real population issues are regional ones associated with the combination of density and poverty. And although intuition may suggest that fewer people would emit lower levels of greenhouse gases, in fact a smaller and richer population may emit higher per capita and higher overall levels.

Voluntary frugality on the scale required to achieve emissions cuts sufficient to stabilize atmospheric concentrations of greenhouse-related gases also seems an unlikely prospect. It would require a voluntary change (many would say sacrifice) on the part of the population of the industrialized world and by the sizeable and powerful elites and professional classes of the less industrialized and industrializing world. It would also require unprecedented restraint on the part of the population already living at humble levels, for them not to take advantage of opportunities to improve their level of comfort. "Human needs and wants" teaches us that regulating consumption is not just a matter of tinkering with tastes. Patterns of spending, even over time, show how, but not why, people make choices in the goods they acquire.

Of course, there are historical precedents for frugality—but none on a large scale that would be compatible with democratic values. Examples abound from anthropology and the history and sociology of religion. But these depend on close personal monitoring by the community to ensure that members do not stray outside of the norms.

Does technology offer a way out? Some think so. Americans in particular are often criticized in European debates for not looking seriously at significant lifestyle changes (although this remains largely talk and little visible action in Europe). If decisionmakers cannot reduce the number of people or the level of goods and satisfaction that people expect, can they not change the way we satisfy demand?

Bottom-up modelers in particular (but not exclusively) point to technology improvements waiting to be taken up, if only the prices were right or some institutional obstacle (e.g., an inconvenient property-right allocation) were not in the way. Unidimensional models such as $I=PAT$ act as if reducing environmental impacts were a strictly linear matter; in fact, the factors that give rise to environmental stress are interrelated in ways that are incompletely understood.

Taken in the aggregate, the Earth's resources can maintain a total population far larger than we presently have or are likely to see in the next century. Similarly, as recounted in "Energy and industry," the technical potential for energy conservation measures is often calculated as very large, and the potential contribution of new technologies to the energy mix is high. The problem is not one of sheer numbers of people relative to the total resource base or available technology, but one of institutional opportunities and constraints, for example, where population is concentrated in environmentally fragile areas or the allocation of resources and entrenched arrangements that favor energy inefficiency and fossil fuels. Both efficiency and fairness play the causal roles in the energy efficiency gap, as they do in poverty and famine.

How governments and other institutions allocate resources is an equity issue. Proposals for theoretically efficient emissions reduction protocols often founder because they are fair only in the sense that they cost least at the macro level. The explicit basis for national and international actions is maximizing utility in macro terms; increasing GNP is not about making the Joneses better off but about making the country as a whole better off, whether or not that means making poor people worse off relative to the rich. Predictably, some people object that they will be disadvantaged disproportionately, and attempts are made to provide resource transfers (financial payments) to compensate such groups.

But equity is not just about how societies distribute resources. It is also the basis for generating social capital—necessary, alongside economic, natural, and intellectual capital, for sustainability. "Cultural discourses" reminds us that the demand for fairness arises out of the establishment of publicly shared expectations for the conduct of community relations. Fairness is integral to the establishment and maintenance of social relations at every level from the micro to the macro, from the local to the global. Because there are differences among the ways in which communities and other institutions organize their social relations, there are differences among the expectations of fairness that people use for judging policy processes and outcomes. In turn, because people everywhere buttress their arguments about what is right by invoking ideas of what is natural, they also exhibit important and sometimes irreconcilable differences in their attitudes to nature as being fragile or robust and in their judgments of vulnerability. Thus, the distribution of ideas of fairness and of nature represent important institutional constraints on the perceived urgency of climate policies as well as of their efficacy and acceptability.

In this way, climate change also provides an arena for debating a wide variety of social, economic, and political issues that society finds difficult to address directly. These include the unequal distribution of wealth within and among nations and the tension between the imperatives of independence and interdependence at all levels of social organization. Much of the debate about equity in climate change mitigation is an extension of the broader debate about international economic development and political empowerment. Clearly, there is a social benefit to be obtained from the existence of an arena in which potential changes in the socioeconomic and political status quo can be explored as deriving from natural imperatives rather than human agency. This enables parties to advance agendas for change without directly and immediately threatening deeply entrenched political and financial interests.

But the situation also presents potential dangers for human society. On the one hand, it is plausible that the opportunity costs of debating significant social and economic change in a surrogate arena may reduce society's capacity to make desirable changes. For example, if policymakers allocate significant economic and political resources to mitigating climate change as a way of enhancing the development of less industrialized countries, they may be reducing the level of resources actually available to fight poverty, hunger, and ignorance. On the other hand, reservations about using the opportunity that a potential natural crisis provides for social and economic reform may lead decisionmakers to ignore or override signals from the natural system that nature is, indeed, about to use its veto over human behavior. It seems that these important questions cannot be addressed directly by policymakers engaged in the climate change discourse as it is currently framed.

Prepare for the likelihood that social, economic, and technological change will be more rapid and have greater direct impacts on human populations than climate change

Climate change is unlikely to determine the fate of human society as a whole. In fact, for much of the world's population, technological, economic, social, and political change is likely to occur at such a rate that changes in the global climate regime of the order anticipated by the IPCC will be barely noticeable. In such a rapidly changing world, long-term environmental issues will find it hard to compete for attention with immediate socioeconomic and political problems and opportunities.

For creating future scenarios, researchers often extrapolate from the present to posit a future that is more of the same. The future world of the IPCC First and Second Assessment Reports is essentially today's world, but more so: more people, more economic growth, and more technology (although largely of the same sort). However, a social-historical perspective suggests that such linear assumptions about global development are highly unrealistic. Looking back, the past century reveals an accelerating rate of social and technical change. An analyst or decisionmaker in 1897 would be have been hard pressed to envisage even the broad outlines of the changes in technological capacity and its distribution over the succeeding 100 years. For example, consider the scale and rapidity of succeeding change in what we now call telecommunications. Commercial telegraphy was introduced in 1844, the telephone in 1878, broadcast radio in 1920, television in 1936; video cameras and recorders, personal computer, cellular phones, and the Internet have all become commonplace in only the past 20 years. The ubiquity of the motor car, the extent of electrification, and popular air travel are all technological developments that were inconceivable to policymakers at the turn of the century. Indeed, Hansard records the concern of a late nineteenth-century British parliamentarian that, at the prevailing rate of emissions, London would be buried several feet deep in horse manure by the 1950s.

Politically, the world at the end of the twentieth century would also have been unrecognizable to a decisionmaker at its birth. The great empires of Britain and France directly dominated Africa and much of Asia, the Austrian Empire remained intact in Europe, and the Russian Empire dominated Europe's eastern edge and northern Asia. Even 50 years ago, the Soviet successors to the Russian imperial mantle seemed unshakably ensconced in the Kremlin, having expanded their influence across all of eastern and central Europe. Economically, the United States had yet to reveal itself as the country that would dominate global markets in the second half of the century. Britain retained its premier position as a world economic leader and as a political force. Socially, women were universally excluded from the popular franchise, where such a franchise existed at all. Slavery had only been abolished in the United States 45 years earlier. Educational opportunities remained limited, even in the richest countries. At the same time as all of these changes compounded each other, who could also have predicted that they would largely pass by such a large segment of the world's population as the poor of the less industrialized countries?

But who can doubt that the paths that humanity will take during the next 100 years will be at least as unpredictable to us now as the past 100 years were even to the most creative minds of the day? While the rate of change is accelerating, the actual direction and specifics of socioeconomic and technical change are inherently unpredictable, severely limiting the usefulness of models and well-understood analogies, if any can be found. In the words attributed to St Paul "whether there be knowledge, it shall vanish away. For we know in part, and we prophesy in part." (1 Corinthians 13)

The rapid rate of socioeconomic and technical change relative to climate change contrasts with the slower background rate of change of the natural world. Ecologists frequently warn that it is not so much the amount of climate change that is dangerous but that it will occur faster than the rate at which ecosystems can adapt. On the other hand, society itself is changing at an accelerating rate. The implications of the rate of climate change for society may therefore be quite different from its implications for unmanaged ecosystems. Not only may societies adapt to climate impacts, but technological change may lead to a more rapid displacement of fossil fuels than is conceivable today. The problem is that there is no way of telling today whether this will prove to be a saving grace or yet another factor compounding the challenge of global environmental governance.

In the best of all possible worlds, decisionmakers responding to the pressures of rapid societal transformation would be able to improve humanity's institutional and technical capacity to deal with slower climate change, at each step along an accelerating path of opportunity. In the worst of worlds, the rapid pace of societal change would distract the attention of decisionmakers from inexorable environmental and resource degradation. To ask, "What is the most likely scenario between these extremes?" is to misunderstand the inherent unpredictability of complex systems over long timescales. We simply cannot predict the future in such a fashion. The authors of "Integrated assessment modeling" point out that the analysts who build integrated assessment models that run for a hundred years are the first to warn that they should not be seen as predictive truth machines.

If decisionmakers cannot predict the unpredictable, how can society face the prospect of profound change occurring at an accelerating pace? To be sure, the answer is not just "Hang on and enjoy or suffer through the ride, depending on your luck." The answer is to build responsive institutional arrangements that monitor change and maximize the flexibility of human populations to respond creatively and constructively to it. However, as we have already seen and will discuss further below, people disagree about what kinds of institutional arrangements are capable of providing such societal resilience.

Recognize the limits of rational planning

The rate and direction of global socioeconomic and technical change over the period in which climate change may be felt is by no means the only significant source of uncertainty affecting public and private sector decisionmakers. Uncertainty is a pervasive condition of policy and decisionmaking. For example, uncertainties predominate in assessing the effects of forestry policy on carbon dioxide emissions and carbon sequestration. Carbon yields in forest plantations vary according to region, species, soil type, precipitation, and management practices. Even in the United States, where land and timber markets are perhaps closer to the economists' ideal market than elsewhere in the world, it is difficult to predict how landowners will respond to various carbon sequestration programs. Finally, the nature of the programmatic and political uncertainty inherent in the development of a carbon sequestration program suggests that models that examine only general policy instruments—taxes and subsidies, allowances and offsets—may not capture some important factors that will determine the effects of the program. Scientific, behavioral, and programmatic uncertainty create a very complex analytic problem. In some cases the uncertainty applies even to the direction of expected change in both the costs of carbon sequestration and the potential accomplishments of the policy. These conditions, more properly characterized as indeterminacy, exacerbate the challenges of designing and implementing appropriate policy options.

As this example illustrates, we do not have a robust description of our own world. We have inaccurate and conflicting theories about how and why people make choices, for themselves and in societies. We model markets well, but nonmarkets only poorly. This is one of the most important limitations on an otherwise very powerful rational tool—cost–benefit analysis. Economists like to evaluate the relative efficacy of many decisions, including decisions on how to manage the environment, in terms of their costs and benefits. "Economic analysis" illustrates how modern cost–benefit analysis reaches beyond the traditional bounds of simple project analysis to investigate optimal provisions of public goods, the efficient level of ambient air and water quality, and other complex environmental issues. Cost–benefit analysis can point to allocations of resources that equate marginal costs with marginal benefits, just like a competitive market; and so promises welfare improvements if not maximization.

However, problems arise when cost–benefit analysis is applied in situations where established and well-behaved markets are not available to provide input values to the calculus (e.g., in the valuation of human life or of unique ecosystems). Like other tools for rational decisionmaking, cost–benefit analysis is widely understood to be valid under a fairly restrictive set of assumptions. These are summarized in "Decision analysis" as a unique decisionmaker faced by a limited number of alternatives which can be compared by an unambiguous quantitative criterion. Provided that violations are minor, decision analysis may still provide a solution that is close to the optimal outcome desired by a rational actor. What is less generally agreed upon is how to distinguish which violations are minor and which are major, as well as what level of cumulative minor violations synergize to invalidate the approach.

For climate change, the same authors recognize significant violations. In particular, there is no single decisionmaker. Differences in values and objectives prevent collectives of decisionmakers from using the same selection criterion for decision alternatives—so decision analysis cannot yield a universally preferred solution. Moreover, uncertainties in climate change are so pervasive and far reaching that the tools for handling uncertainty provided by decision analysis are no longer sufficient.

Cost–benefit analysis is also subject to dispute on the part of stakeholders who do not subscribe to the value of efficiency that underpins it. The focus of economists over the past 10 years has been on efficient policy instruments to affect prices and encourage more ecologically sustainable choices. These analyses and recommendations are presented as purely technical contributions to rational decisionmaking. However, as we have described in Chapter 2, they are more than mere technical exercises. Ultimately they rely for their persuasiveness on their commitment to efficiency as an underlying driving value. But cost–benefit analyses have met with dogged political resistance from stakeholders committed to values other than efficiency which were not taken into account in the analysis. The limitations of rational analysis and planning are often hard to accept in the face of three centuries of commitment to the ". . . absolute belief that the solution to our problems must be a more determined application of rationally organized expertise." (Saul 1992: 8)

Currently there is strong interest among policy analysts in stimulating appropriate technology. Again, this raises fundamental problems of indeterminacy for policymakers, highlighted in "Technological change." Governments cannot call desirable technologies into being or maturity by legislation. Incentives and constraints (including regulation) do have effects, but governments cannot gauge their content and timing. In addition, governments have little knowledge of technological possibilities; they act on the basis of technological promises. This leads to a control problem: in principle, governments have the greatest influence over technological choices when they know the least about the impacts and desirability of the technology; when the technology is fully developed and widely used, it is extremely difficult to control it (because of vested interests and high adjustment costs).

This dilemma of knowledge and control applies to all actors involved in technological development. Indeed, technology is continually shaped by actors who exert themselves to domesticate and control the technology, with varying degrees of success. Technology is not out of control, but the complex dynamics of attempts to rationally steer technological change often do not lead to expected or acceptable outcomes. Again the limitations on rational analysis and planning are revealed. But this does not mean that a worthwhile technology policy is beyond our grasp, merely that it cannot be based solely on rational prediction and the assessment of cost–benefit efficiency. The recognition that greenhouse gas emissions result from myriad interactions among population, consumption, and technology can lead to different approaches to managing climate change. Each element, far from being a driving factor to be controlled with a policy lever, is a different entrance point from which to view a landscape of interwoven actions; each is a different dimension of the same complex set of conditions, and none by itself has the potential to transform human society.

As we draw on fundamental understanding of processes of technological development, we can identify and define opportunities for productive intervention in the process. "Technological change" suggests that we should view policy intervention as the modulation rather than the direction of technological development. Government intervention should therefore be oriented toward the strategic interactions among the different actors, rather than laying down functional requirements. Government should intervene to change the processes involved in technology development: facilitating communication, broadening the scope of inquiry, supporting participants that might not otherwise be heard, providing resources for research unlikely to yield short-term results, and stimulating cooperative activities in a novelty-seeking business environment. For example, government can secure a future market for a new product. Or in the case of technological controversies, government can facilitate discussions among interested parties, to generate better understanding of the issues, and guide technology developers in their decisions. Thus, the role of the government is that of facilitator seeking to align other actors in the process of change rather than that of a regulator directing technology choices.

For climate change, it is as important to shift the hydrocarbon-based energy regime as it is to develop particular new technologies and systems. Just as technological trajectories branch and shift, so can policymakers think of a transition path toward a new regime and apply themselves to bring this about. Technologies grow in niches—protected spaces for further evolution without the full force of selection being felt. Policymakers can actively create such niches and manage the process so as to reduce the extent of protection gradually. Positive feedback through interactive learning and institutional adaptation occurs and, by creating a little irreversibility in the right direction, the transition process is pushed forward.

As a policy instrument, strategic niche management promotes technical change in directions that offer both short-term and long-term benefits. But, success is not guaranteed; it is an example of a heuristic approach, exploiting points of attachment in an evolving sociotechnical landscape. On the other hand, by drawing on our understanding of the nature and dynamics of technological development, it definitely is a realistic approach.

What, then, can policymakers do? They can search for points of intervention—various points of end-use, energy production, extraction, for example—instead of designing grand solutions. In the words of the protagonist of Graham Swift's novel *Waterland* (1983: 336):

It's progress if you can stop the world slipping away. My humble model for progress is the reclamation of land. Which is repeatedly, never-endingly retrieving what is lost. A dogged vigilant business. A dull yet valuable business. A hard inglorious business. But you shouldn't go mistaking the reclamation of land for the building of empires.

Policymakers can encourage niches, protect them for a while, allow competition while preserving alternative paths. They can perform such nonmarket roles as engaging interest in new technologies, sponsoring focused R&D, and encouraging information exchange. They can work indirectly to build and strengthen resilience. They can resist the temptation to be linear and direct in their desire to manage problems. This approach, admittedly incrementalist, is sometimes dismissed as lacking understanding of root causes—but we have seen that appeals to root causes (such as population growth or overconsumption) are most usually rhetorical rallying cries of particular cultural or interest groups and that, in any case, consensus on causes is not a precondition for effective collective action.

Employ the full range of analytic perspectives and decision aids from the natural and social sciences and the humanities in climate change policymaking

Despite the early and concerted efforts of some leading natural scientists to broaden the range of tools used to understand climate change issues, climate change decisionmaking has been dominated by natural science and macro-economic perspectives. The social science viewpoint brings into focus important issues; that is, policymakers can literally see things differently, things that are invisible or pushed into the background when viewed from a natural science standpoint. The social sciences focus on human systems that allow and constrain choices, systems that bound what people can do about climate change and other global changes. From this viewpoint, the physical processes are in the background, although their importance remains. The trick to master is seeing both perspectives and finding paths forward that account for both environmental and social constraints and opportunities.

In the late 1980s there was much rending of garments about the compatibility of natural and social science research on global environmental change. However, *Human choice and climate change* finds that they are able to accommodate each other rather comfortably, albeit in a limited fashion, by exchanging information between natural and social science assessments of the stocks and flows of goods and materials represented by the boxes and arrows of flow charts and systems diagrams. The harder challenge is integrating this kind of social science with another kind of social science, the interpretive tradition, which is historically and methodologically closer to the humanities (see Ch. 2).

We have demonstrated in *Human choice and climate change* that incorporation of the insights of the interpretive social sciences can greatly expand understanding of the human dimensions of climate change and decisionmaking, ranging from the production and evaluation of scientific knowledge to the negotiation and implementation of policy at international, national, and local levels.

For example, social studies of science as described in "Science and decisionmaking" can help both natural scientists and decisionmakers (the rest of us) in evaluating climate change science by bringing the social processes by which science is produced out of the black box. This process is not congenial to some scientists, who are sensitive to any suggestion that social factors shape their theories, methods, data, or results. Some social scientists have deliberately steered social science research programs away from looking at the process of creating climate science, for fear of offending potential collaborators from the natural sciences. But concern that social science studies of knowledge production are somehow antiscientific is misguided. We should neither pretend that any body of knowledge is value free, nor that we can dismiss that knowledge merely by exposing its assumptions and value framework. Similarly, studying the social processes involved in forming a scientific consensus and extending that consensus to affect social decisionmaking does not invalidate the science. Such studies can help policymakers to avoid overstating scientific findings (and thus avoid backlash) and to see what is needed to establish scientific knowledge as a basis for institutional action.

In fact, in relation to the most important scientific assessment of climate change science, that of the IPCC, social science analysis suggests that despite some valid criticisms related to participation of less industrialized countries and representation of a sufficiently broad spectrum of social science, the principal findings of the IPCC may be regarded as robust. Interpretive social science therefore offers little comfort either to those who would dismiss scientific warnings about changing climate or to those who would prefer to preserve science from public scrutiny. With respect to public scrutiny, the openness of the IPCC to nongovernmental organizations (NGOs) represents a significant step in the direction of creating at the international level the kind of vernacular, civic, or postnormal science envisaged by the authors of various contributions to Volumes 1–3, including "Science and decisionmaking," "Cultural discourses," "Institutions for political action," "Coastal zones and oceans," "Energy and society," "Economic Analysis," "Decision analysis," and "Integrated assessment."

Nevertheless, social scientists should beware of the immigration effect by which the most recent group to establish itself in a new country seeks to bar the door behind it and exclude the next in line. In addition to philosophical perspectives on what is right, what is natural, and what is beautiful, the humanities also offer potentially valuable input to decision processes and opportunities for cultural learning, the creation, transmission, and interpretation of new meanings of nature and society, and of the relationships between them. What societies celebrate in literature, art, and performance publicly expresses and communicates shared hopes, fears, and expectations about the world in which climate change is experienced. "Cultural discourses" and "Reasoning by analogy" remind us that storytelling is one of the most important ways that humans construct their individual and collective identities. Hence, history and mythology can tell us much about ourselves, our values, and our behavior in relation to climate, lifestyle, and human development. Bridging the gap between descriptive and interpretive social sciences potentially reunites the full range of human capabilities that were rent asunder by the Enlightenment. To cope with global challenges, such as climate change, the greatest and least of decisionmakers will be better armed by accessing their full range of capabilities for understanding and choosing.

This kind of analytic capability requires a complex balance among disciplinary, multidisciplinary, and interdisciplinary activities. Disciplinary researchers are spinners who weave intellectual threads for interdisciplinary weavers who make them into whole cloth. Neither can exist without the other. But the appropriate balance of disciplinary, multidisciplinary, and interdisciplinary research cannot be achieved and sustained by the research community without the support of public and private sector decisionmakers and evidence that the multiple perspectives provided by the full range of research perspectives are used and valued in decisionmaking.

Even interdisciplinary research and analysis remains the province of intellectual elites. There is a further step beyond interdisciplinarity that should be considered, that is, to expand traditional concepts of expertise by developing institutions of civic science that combine universal scientific expertise with the local expertise and craft skills of stakeholders in decisionmaking. Embracing a broad range of expertise in this way takes analysis and decisionmaking beyond the traditional expert/lay dichotomy which in any case obscures significant variation in the perceptions and preferences of both. It also obscures the fact that real people are not consistently experts or lay people. There are no universal experts and, in the civic arena, even the most modest lay person has some relevant expertise. Relevant knowledge brought to bear in the climate discourses is not composed solely of scientific facts about climate chemistry, dynamics, and impacts, but also derives from various experiences of social change and societal responses to natural change.

The expert/lay dichotomy also structures communication as a unidirectional process in which expert knowledge is passed to the public either to alleviate its ignorance or redress its misperceptions. In this mode, decisionmakers are often stopped in their tracks by recalcitrant populations who rightly insist that they have not been heard and that their expertise (what anthropologists call local knowledge) has been ignored. The suggestion in both "Science and decisionmaking" and "Cultural discourses," that expert discourses are structured by the same elements of social organization as lay discourses, redirects efforts at communication from simply overcoming ignorance to creating shared frames of reference and opportunities for shared action. Public information campaigns, which assume that discrepancies between lay and expert accounts of climate change are simply attributable to knowledge deficiencies, are bound to fail. Effective communication about climate change issues requires understanding of the frames of reference being used by all participants.

Design policy instruments for real world conditions rather than try to make the world conform to a particular policy model

The model most used by social scientists and policymakers to account for the difficulty of changing human behavior is that of barriers to information. The idea can be conveyed by a hydraulic metaphor in which water (information or technology) runs down a mountain (diffuses or is disseminated). If a channel is blocked, water backs up or is diverted. If the barrier is removed, water (information) flows freely. People make bad choices because of poor price signals (lack of information or misinformation that blocks true information). If prices signal the true costs, then the barrier to behavioral change is removed and people will do the right thing. Although this model works nicely in well-behaved markets with many traders having access to full information, it does not provide useful guidance for communication and policy implementation under many of the conditions that influence emissions-related behavior and opportunities for adaptation.

The hydrologic model of information flows comes under critical scrutiny in several chapters of *Human choice and climate change*, most explicitly in "Energy and society," "Decision analysis," and "Cultural discourses." The model lacks the required focus on meaning. Its continued use obscures the difficulties of creating a global-scale framework for changing human relationships to the environment (and of necessity with each other). It also obscures the availability of opportunities that can be found beyond the rational actor paradigm, presuming that, if the implementation process is not going according to plan, the fault must be in user distortions that can be fixed. The model masquerades as facilitative when it is really prescriptive. Instead of trying to make the world conform to the normative tenets of the rational choice model, we should attempt to understand how decisions really are made (outside of well-behaved markets) and shape information pertinent to decisionmakers and their available options.

With respect to policy implementation, most analyses focus on the impact of emissions reductions policies on the energy sectors of industrialized countries. The bounding conditions for such analyses bear some reasonable resemblance to the idealized models of economic theory. For the most part, fossil energy fuels are fungible and, especially for stationary energy uses, they are highly substitutable for one another. They are consumed in reliable and predictable ways. Especially in the industrialized countries, they are widely traded in well-established markets, where information is plentiful and prices are responsive to fairly uniform trading opportunities.

Even under these conditions, industrialized countries exhibit significant variation in the presence of those characteristics that could be considered ideal for the successful application of climate policy instruments such as regulations, taxes, and information programs. These attributes are listed in "Institutions for political action" as including:

- a well-developed institutional infrastructure to implement regulation
- an economy likely to respond well to fiscal policy instruments because it possesses certain characteristics of economic models of the free market
- a highly developed information industry and mass communications infrastructure, for educating, advertising, and jawboning
- a vast combined private and public annual R&D budget for reducing uncertainties and establishing pilot programs.

To the extent that these close-to-ideal institutional conditions for conventional policy implementation are missing, policymakers may expect to encounter further obstacles to the effectiveness of policy instruments. This situation is exacerbated in the case of policies addressing land and water use, which are key not only to carbon sequestration policies but also to most adaptive strategies such as migration, crop switching, and changes in the design of buildings and human settlements.

It is much more difficult to analyze the effects of policy instruments in circumstances where these close-to-ideal circumstances do not pertain:

- where emissions information is less reliable, such as in the forestry sector
- where market conditions are much less ideal or even nonexistent, as in important segments of the economies of less industrialized countries
- where political conditions give rise to uncertainty over the sustainability of the policy program
- where policies focus on highly uncertain adaptation strategies rather than on emissions.

Less industrialized countries often have poor infrastructures to begin with, a problem exacerbated by a lack of human, financial, and technological resources. In addition, these countries are likely to be focused on more basic and fundamental considerations of nation building and economic development. Environmental issues can be low on their scale of priorities.

The harsh reality is that many less industrialized countries face a serious problem of scarce resources to carry out the most elementary functions of government. Competition among state agencies for whatever resources are available inevitably leaves environmental protection and natural resource management agencies without the necessary investment to establish effective monitoring and implementation programs. The shortage of program resources is exacerbated by pressures to exploit natural resources to earn foreign income, increasing demands of the population for energy, and pressures to convert forest land to agriculture and human habitation. Under the combined weight of all these factors, the issue of optimizing across regulations, taxes, permits, education, and demonstration projects becomes academic.

Lack of implementation infrastructure may be the largest single obstacle to effective policies, especially under the frontier conditions of Amazonia and other areas of tropical deforestation. These are situations where prior claims of indigenous populations are nonexistent or disregarded, and where the ability to monitor behavior, settle disputes, and enforce rules and contracts lies with individuals and groups possessing the power to coerce. Unfortunately, conventional development approaches tend to dismiss these characteristics of the society as mere details of implementation when, in fact, they represent fundamental structural differences between frontier societies and those where the institutions of civil society, essential to the functioning of regulatory regimes or efficient markets, are either severely curtailed or altogether absent.

In principle, the economic conditions of less industrialized countries also present opportunities to achieve emissions reductions at lower absolute cost than in the industrialized nations that have already made capital intensive commitments to fossil fuel technologies and may lack the land resources available for carbon sequestration programs. The solution is to design information to fit the frameworks of meaning that are relevant to stakeholders and to design policy instruments to suit specific conditions. "One-size-fits-all" seldom fits at all.

Incorporate climate change concerns into other, more immediate issues such as employment, defense, economic development, and public health

Wherever climate policies are pursued, effective actions designed to mitigate or respond opportunistically or adaptively to climate change are likely to be those that are most fully integrated into more general policy strategies for economic and social development. The more that climate change issues are routinized as part of the planning perspective at the appropriate level of implementation (e.g., the firm or the community), the more likely they are to achieve desired goals. Climate policies as such are bound to be hard to implement. This conclusion recasts the issue of compliance and implementation in important and challenging ways. As analysis moves beyond the idea of a rational instrumental framework of evaluation, decision, and implementation to a continuous framework of interactive negotiation, policy explicitly becomes the formalization of actions being undertaken by participating parties.

However, mere piggybacking of climate change onto an existing political agenda as another stick to wave at political opponents is unlikely to succeed. Likewise, dressing up climate change measures as the means to pursue higher taxation or welfare expenditure is also likely to run into substantial opposition. There are no easy answers, as true win–win solutions continue to prove elusive. So far, it must be said that no country has seriously addressed the reduction of its greenhouse gases as a matter of genuine commitment. Those that have tried to do so (e.g., Denmark, Norway, and the Netherlands) have encountered serious impediments in the economic lobbies of industry and transportation—so much so that even these environmentally motivated countries have had to back off. Unless and until climate change is perceived as a real economic threat with major consequences for the stability of future trading partners, and until there is a collective will to map a common trajectory to agreed limits, then climate change will produce plenty of rhetorical hot air, but little concerted action.

Without a major policy stimulus (such as a significant carbon tax) or an unmistakable signal that climate change is real and threatening, any country is likely to delay the kinds of behavioral changes that would be necessary to arrest the process. "Institutions for political action" indicates that issues that are perceived by governments to be on the policy periphery, such as climate change, are not easily factored into consideration of issues at the policy core such as national economic policy or corporate manufacturing strategy. In addition, policies such as carbon taxes, explicitly formulated to address issues on the policy periphery, are likely to be carefully scrutinized for potential adverse effects on the policy core by its institutional stewards. For example, the issue networks and policy communities around environmental ministries in most countries have been shown to be weak relative to those around economic and defense ministries. In no case has climate change been perceived within the powerful ministries and their policy communities as sufficiently threatening to their departmental interests to disrupt their existing policy agendas.

Clearly, climate change either has to be shown to be a compelling threat that overshadows other policy demands, or it has to be integrated into the routinized decisionmaking frameworks of government organizations and agencies whose primary policy concerns (such as finance and energy) are widely recognized as compelling. The appropriate response therefore is to incorporate climate concerns into the everyday concerns of people at the local level and the big concerns of policymakers at the national level. At the moment the research agendas of either the natural or social sciences provide little help or guidance for this. A combination of the focus on emissions (rather than, say, vulnerability) with the speaking-truth-to-power model of analysis and policymaking is producing least knowledge where it could do most good, that is at the levels of households, firms, and communities. Once again, the need identified in several chapters— for a new model of cooperative action by scientists, policymakers, and other stakeholders—would be appropriate.

Joining climate change issues to issues of societal resilience opens the agenda to a broad range of focus areas, including economic development, institutional restructuring, provision of multiple strategies, fostering civil society, and strengthening indigenous arrangements (e.g., land tenure) that are working. Resilience encompasses not just preservation from harm (where this is possible) but also strengthening or establishing alternative economic activities (both market and nonmarket) and social structures.

Take a regional and local approach to climate policymaking and implementation

Although national politics are important, they may obscure another fundamental reason why, even when a climate policy is accepted (as in the Netherlands), it nevertheless proves to be remarkably ineffective. Analysts and policymakers continue to focus their attention at the level of the nation state, whether their focus is on the ability of states to develop solidarity with one another or to create appropriate frameworks of political and economic solidarity to implement their policy goals domestically. However, in most cases, the state is actually very far removed from the sources of emissions. The policy levers of the state therefore, have to be very long to reach the locus of desired action. All too often, especially, although by no means exclusively, in the less industrialized world, the levers of state power are not connected to anything at all at the local level, where policies must be implemented by ordinary people living in face-to-face communities.

There is much variation around the world in the relationship of national to provincial and local governments. However, in the day-to-day lives of most people in the world, local government is the more salient political actor. It delivers or withholds essential services; it mediates between the citizen and the nation state through local officials, such as police officers, who may have to monitor vehicle emissions, or building inspectors, responsible for seeing that new construction meets energy efficiency standards. Furthermore, over 50 percent of the world's population now live in urban areas, contributing a significant portion of global emissions of greenhouse gases. The density, mixture, and physical layout of residential and commercial neighborhoods all influence the energy intensity of the community. Yet many of these factors are more directly under the control of community governments than of national ministries.

Already cities around the world are networking with one another at the level of municipal administrations and citizen activists, and without the intermediation of national authorities. For example, urban leaders met at the Municipal Leaders' Summit for Climate Change in New York in 1993 to establish the Cities

For Climate Protection program. This program was an extension of an earlier initiative linking 14 cities in the United States, Canada, Europe, and Turkey, designed to strengthen local commitment to reduce urban greenhouse gas emissions, to research and develop best practices in pilot communities, to share planning tools and experiences, and to enhance ties among municipalities across national boundaries, especially between those in industrialized and less industrialized countries.

"Institutions for political action" argues that the bulk of climate change politics may have to devolve to the local level, if policies are to become effective in the informal institutional dynamics of individuals and households. The rise of informal networks of cooperation is an important development here, spurred on via schools and colleges, various social groupings, and local businesses. Whether policy innovation and behavioral change are led locally or nationally, they will be marked by a process of institutional learning that either moves current peripheral concerns about climate change to the core of people's daily concerns or, at least, palpably and convincingly links climate policies to these everyday concerns.

A significant problem is that almost all of the climate change policy research and analysis is aimed at high-level policymakers. Funding agencies tend to be those of national governments or of NGOs seeking to influence government policy or international negotiations. Although this research is important, it is not very helpful to a city manager, the general manager of an aluminum smelter, the operator of a regional reservoir system, or a householder seeking guidance on how to do the right thing for the climate at the same time as doing the best for his or her citizens, stockholders and employees, consumers, or family members.

Direct resources to identifying vulnerability and promoting resilience, especially where the impacts will be largest

Whatever the level at which decisions are made, sustainability is about being nimble, not about being right. Policymakers should balance their current emphasis on linear goal-setting and implementation by paying more attention to promoting societal resilience through enhanced capability for strategy switching. This is particularly urgent where populations are vulnerable to the early impacts of climate change.

As the authors of "Coastal zones and oceans" point out, central problems in this high-minded endeavor are to define vulnerability and resilience and to identify relevant markers or indicators of each. For example, industrialized countries seem to be vulnerable to violent storms in terms of physical infrastructure but not in terms of human lives, whereas the opposite vulnerabilities characterize less industrialized countries. The IPCC methodology for assessing vulnerability in coastal zones focused on people, land, and infrastructure at risk, arriving at quantitative estimates for each. In "Reasoning by analogy," vulnerability is defined by negative impacts of a climate event on particular societies; included in the vulnerability assessment are political and economic systems, and other institutional arrangements. Changes in regional patterns of habitability would exacerbate existing problems for poor populations living in environmentally vulnerable areas, such as low-lying tropical regions. Here we may anticipate that more poor people will go hungry, get sick, and die young.

Human activities and groups are sensitive to climate to the degree that they can be affected by it, vulnerable to the degree that they can be harmed. A resilient system, activity, or population is one with low vulnerability: either resistant to hazard effects or readily capable of coping with and recovering from them. Vulnerability should be distinguished from hazards—defined as events threatening people and things that they value, or the probability of the occurrence of such events. Impacts are the actual consequences (losses or, conceivably, gains) resulting from a biophysical event. Negative impacts are the product of hazard events and vulnerability. A focus on vulnerability, then, is a partial one that addresses the sensitivity of human systems only to the threats, and not also to the opportunities, presented by particular climatic anomalies and by the human activities with which they interact. There are few studies of gains from climate variation and of human activities vulnerable to climate that compare the losses to the overall gains from the activity. Yet "the use of resources of a hazardous area almost always leads to social benefits as well as social costs. It is essential to identify the tradeoffs between the benefits and the costs in the broadest sense" (Burton et al. 1993: 188).

The vulnerability of populations and activities is the most widely used umbrella concept for those factors that mediate between geophysical events and human losses. Because vulnerability and its causes play an essential role in determining impacts, understanding the dynamics of vulnerability is as important as monitoring and predicting climate change and interannual variation. Vulnerability draws attention to the amplifiers or attenuators of the impacts of climate change and channels them toward certain groups, certain institutions, and certain places. It also emphasizes the degree to which the risks of climate catastrophe can be cushioned or ameliorated by adaptive actions that are or can be brought within the reach of populations at risk.

In comparing the vulnerability of populations, researchers distinguish between differences in physical exposure to the hazardous agent and different abilities to cope with its impacts. The former are closely associated with biophysical, and the latter with socioeconomic, differentiation. Aspects of the biophysical environment may be important sources of coping ability, for instance, and differences in exposure to hazards may be the consequence of socioeconomic differences. No standard framework exists for identifying different sources of vulnerability, but clearly they are many and complex. Poverty is generally recognized as one of the most important correlates of vulnerability to hazard, but it is neither necessary nor sufficient for it. The very young and the old are often identified as especially vulnerable. Other categories widely invoked are differences in health, gender, ethnicity, education, and experience with the hazard in question. Empirical local-level studies reveal such complex mosaics of vulnerability as to cast doubt upon attempts to describe patterns and estimate trends at the global or even the regional scale. Vulnerability to global climate change is likely to be as complex.

The IPCC Second Assessment Report has made a preliminary identification of regions and societies where climate change impacts are likely to be most severe, for example, coastal zones and areas that are already warm and dry. Natural science indicates that the impacts will be felt in regions that are geographically exposed (e.g., low-lying tropical regions).

However, policymakers should be wary of comparable vulnerability league tables and broad pronouncements. Some researchers argue that the industrialized world is more vulnerable because of increasing interdependencies and rigidities in the industrial system and its supporting infrastructures. Other researchers have argued that the vulnerability of the less industrialized world is greater because of its immediate dependence on agriculture. The emphasis should be on collaborations wherever gains can be made in increasing the capacities of societies to deal with problems that may result from climate change and other environmental changes (e.g., water and air pollution, overfishing). When all is said and done, building both the social and financial capital of the poor may be their best defense.

Use a pluralistic approach to decisionmaking

The FCCC provides an important symbolic framework expressive of worldwide concern about climate and about the persistent issues of global development that are inextricably bound up with it. However, "Institutions for political action" suggests that smaller, often less formal, agreements among states; states and firms; and firms, NGOs, and communities may provide the vehicle for effective climate change responses. This process may appear to be irrational and conflictual, but the potential exists to make the most of diversity and the variety of decision strategies that diversity offers to decisionmakers.

At the international level, governments are presently keeping a tight grip on their prerogatives to represent their respective national interests in climate negotiations, whereas domestically the interests that are represented as national are shaped by the interaction of policy networks, including bureaucracies, businesses, and citizen groups. At this level, institutionalized patterns of behavior currently tend to give the business sector a privileged position; other interest groups may find they are deflected from the locus of decision-making by their inability to penetrate institutionalized patterns of consultation and representation. Still other demands—those made by the Deep Greens, for example—may simply go unheard because they are not considered legitimate or appropriate by network gatekeepers.

However, although it is undoubtedly true that the institutional structure is biased in favor of some groups (and that others may be effectively prevented from entering the political arena and even prevented from articulating their concerns by acts of conscious and unconscious exclusion), it would be quite wrong to portray institutionalized patterns of domination as being immutable. Even the weakest and most disenfranchised can find the means to influence the activities of the strong.

Policymakers must look across several different dimensions simultaneously. For example, Figure 4.1 encapsulates:

- timescale: short, medium, and long terms
- spatial scale: local, national/regional, and global
- institutional actor: markets, governments, and civil society.

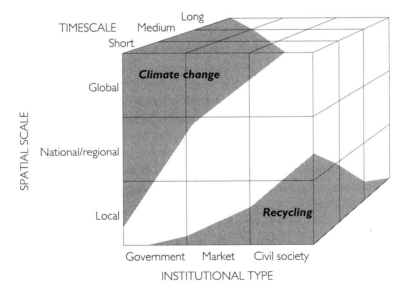

Figure 4.1   Policy opportunities are multidimensional.

135

Most research efforts, and indeed most policymaking efforts, focus on a single element from each dimension. Presently, climate change policy activity is concentrated in only a small part of the three-dimensional space that defines potential policy activities. For example, the FCCC focuses on immediate goals to reduce emissions at the global (and, to some extent, national) levels within the formal institutions of a market-oriented worldview. (In contrast, most recycling efforts are short-term local programs using networks within a market orientation.) However, there is little or no articulation or linkage among different timescales, levels, worldview, and institutional structures. To connect these elements (which, after all, is the implementation task) requires two explicit recognitions:

- Articulation from global to local levels and from formal to informal institutional structures is mediated by codes, standards (including scientific standards), rules of thumb, and professional and indigenous practice (see Shapiro 1997).
- The design of policy must include implementation paths that accommodate different worldviews, institutional structures, levels, and timescales.

Policymaking that links the local and global levels requires extension of civic life, both as civic science (linking scientific and technical knowledge with local knowledge and craft skills) and civic society (associational links outside of governments and markets) at all levels to complement the market and government. It also requires extending integrated assessment analysis and inquiry, specifically scientific efforts to provide information useful to decisionmakers at all levels—not only global and national, but also firms, NGOs, and households.

Conclusion

The authors of *Human choice and climate change* have suggested that public and private sector decisionmakers adjust their approaches to climate policy in some important respects. We have advocated for increased attention to adaptation strategies. We have called for a stronger focus on institutional constraints affecting both the implementation of adaptation and mitigation policies. We have argued for shifting the balance of climate change policies from optimizing approaches to mitigation toward building resilience and flexibility into societies. We have spoken in favor of analytic and decisionmaking approaches that focus on integrating climate change concerns into existing sectoral and local priorities. We have argued that special attention should be paid to understanding vulnerability, especially among the poor and already vulnerable. In so doing we have consistently stressed a participatory approach in which decisions emanate from as low down the political hierarchy as possible. Among these mechanisms, the call for civic science has been recurrent.

But we recognize that making this kind of high-minded advice operational is beset with difficulties. Not least among these is that, in putting this advice into practice, public and private sector decisionmakers are likely to encounter stakeholders who advocate other approaches or who interpret the approaches advocated here in different ways. Among the first group, one can expect to find the precautionary coalition that currently directs the policy focus on targets and timetables for emissions reductions. It is important to recognize that strong champions of targeted mitigation are not the enemies of our suggested approach, but part of it. They play an essential role in continually drawing the attention of an inattentive society to the issues of climate change. Their somewhat inflexible approach to emissions reduction highlights the importance of weaning the world away from a hydrocarbon economy. Our approach differs from theirs in that we place a counterbalancing weight on the pressing social welfare issues that, from a climate policy viewpoint, seem to be forever getting in the way of radical action.

We also expect significant differences in interpretation and operational priorities among those who embrace our agenda. For example, we have just discussed important differences of opinion about how to determine and measure or rank vulnerability. We know that people operating with different myths of nature and society as fragile, robust, or resilient within limits are likely to have very different interpretations of both vulnerability and what constitutes resilience in the face of vulnerability. In these situations, to ask which view is right is already to miss the point. The first essential for policy in a complex world is to resist the urge to declare one viewpoint true and to reject others. Resisting this temptation is not mindless relativism that says one idea is just as good as any other. That would be a recipe for passivity and the abdication of choice. If all paths are equally good or bad, why choose at all? Our view could not be further from this. But where there is contestation about either the way the world (natural and social) actually works or about the way the world ought to work, policymakers are likely to find themselves facing competing partial truths. To commit oneself, one's family, firm, community, or nation to just one of these viewpoints is to gamble that it will turn out to be right and the others wrong. It is far more likely that all will be partly right and all will be partly wrong. Recognizing this and stewarding the kind of institutional pluralism necessary to maintain multiple viewpoints and a rich repertoire of policy strategies from which to choose is what promoting societal resilience, sustainable development, and climate change governance is all about.

References

Burton, I., R. W. Kates, G. F. White 1993. *The environment as hazard*, 2nd edn. New York: Guilford Press.

Saul, J. R. 1992. *Voltaire's bastards: the dictatorship of reason in the West*. Ontario: Viking Penguin.

Shapiro, S. 1997. Degrees of freedom: the interaction of standard practice and engineering judgment. *Science, Technology, and Human Values* **22**(3), 286–316.

Swift, G. 1983. *Waterland*. New York: Vintage International.

Key data on human activity
and climate change

The dimensions of the climate change issue can be captured descriptively by data on changes in population, economic activity (including energy use), and greenhouse-related emissions. Such data allow scientists and policymakers to scope potential problems and explore strategies to manage human activities in the future.

Population

Year	Billions
1850	1.26
1990	5.262
1990 OECD	0.859
1990 non-OECD	4.403
2100 projections	6–18
2100 OECD projections	1–1.5
2100 non-OECD projections	5–16.5

Economic activity

GNP and year	Billion dollars
1850 world	882 Geary–Khamis dollars
1990 world	US$20866
1990 OECD	US$16356
1990 non-OECD	US$4510
2100 world projections	US$78000–540000
2100 OECD projections	US$32000–180000
2100 non-OECD projections	US$46000–360000

Energy

Energy consumption	
1850 world	30 EJ
1990 world	375 EJ
1990 OECD	175 EJ
1990 non-OECD	200 EJ
2100 world projections	500–2500 EJ
2100 OECD projections	150–500 EJ
2100 non-OECD projections	350–2000 EJ

Greenhouse gas emissions and concentrations

Percentage of 1990 change in radiative forcing accounted for by gas	
Carbon dioxide (CO_2)	115
Methane (CH_4)	34
Nitrous oxide (N_2O)	11
Chlorofluorocarbons (CFCs) & CFC substitutes	8
Tropospheric ozone	30
Sulfur (S)	−84
Biomass aerosols	−15
Concentration of CO_2 in the atmosphere	
1850	275 ppmv (±5 ppmv)
1994	358 ppmv (760 PgC)
Stock of CO_2 (1994)	
In biota	550 PgC
In soils	550 PgC
Anthropogenic emissions per year	
1850	
Fossil fuel	>0.1 PgC (+10%)
Cement manufacture	0.0 PgC
Land-use	0.5 PgC (+100%)
1990	
Fossil fuel	6.0 PgC (+10%)
Cement manufacture	0.1 PgC (+100%)
Land-use	1.3 PgC (+100%)
2100 projections	
Fossil fuel	20 PgC (6 to 75 PgC)
Land-use emissions	0 PgC (−1 to 3 PgC)
Fossil fuel resource base	> 10000 PgC
Cumulative emissions for various CO_2 concentration ceilings	
1990–2100	
450 ppmv	714 PgC
550 ppmv	1043 PgC
650 ppmv	1239 PgC
750 ppmv	1348 PgC

References

1990 population
World Bank 1993. *World development report.* New York: Oxford University Press (for the World Bank).
MSPA 1997. Data Bank of World Development Statistics [diskette]. Washington DC: World Bank.

1990 GDP
World Bank 1993. *World development report.* New York: Oxford University Press (for the World Bank).
UNDP 1993. *Human development report.* New York: Oxford University Press (for the United Nations Development Program).
Facts & Maps, ver.1.0; GDP expressed in 1990 $US at market exchange rates.

1990 energy consumption
OECD 1997. Energy Balances and Energy Statistics [diskette]. Paris: International Energy Agency.

2100 population and GNP
Houghton, J. T., L. G. Meira Filho, H. Lee, B. A. Callander, E. Haites, N. Harris, K. Maskell (eds) 1995. *Climate change 1994: radiative forcing of climate change & an evaluation of the IS92 scenarios.* Cambridge: Cambridge University Press. GNP estimates using growth rates from table 6.3; population estimates from table 6.4 (shared out by region)

Radiative forcing values for 1990
Wigley, T. M. L. & Raper, S. C. B. 1992. Implications for climate and sea level of revised IPCC emissions scenarios. *Nature* **357**, 293–300.

1850 world population
United Nations 1973. *The determinants and consequences of population trends,* vol. 1. New York: United Nations.

1850 world GNP
Expressed in million Geary–Khamis dollars; linearly interpolated given 1820 and 1870 data from Maddison, A. 1995. *Monitoring the world economy 1820–1992.* Paris: OECD.

1850 energy consumption
Estimated from data in IIASA and World Energy Council 1995. *Global energy perspectives to 2050 and beyond.* London: World Energy Council.

2100 energy consumption
Leggett, J., W. J. Pepper, R. J. Swart, J. Edmonds, L. G. Meira Filho, I. Mintzer, M. X. Wang, J. Wasson 1992. Emissions scenarios for the IPCC: an update. In *Climate change 1992: the supplementary report to the IPCC scientific assessment,* J. T. Houghton, B. A. Callander, S. K. Varney (eds). Cambridge: Cambridge University Press.

Sponsoring organizations, International Advisory Board, and project participants

INSTITUTIONAL SPONSORS AND COLLABORATORS

Pacific Northwest National Laboratory (PNNL), USA

US Department of Energy (DOE), USA

Electric Power Research Institute (EPRI), USA

Economic and Social Research Council (ESRC), UK

International Institute for Applied Systems Analysis (IIASA), Austria

National Institute for Public Health and Environment (RIVM), Netherlands

Korean Energy Economics Institute (KEEI), Korea

National Oceanic and Atmospheric Administration (NOAA), USA

Centre for Social and Economic Research on the Global Environment (CSERGE), UK

LOS-Senteret, Norway

Musgrave Institute, UK

Centre for the Study of Environmental Change (CSEC), UK

Potsdam Institute for Climate Impacts Research (PIK), Germany

Swiss Federal Institute for Environmental Science and Technology (EAWAG), Switzerland

Commonwealth Scientific and Industrial Research Organization (CSIRO), Australia

Research Institute of Innovative Technology for the Earth (RITE), Japan

THE INTERNATIONAL ADVISORY BOARD

Dr Francisco Barnes

The Honorable Richard Benedick

Professor Harvey Brooks

Professor the Lord Desai of St Clement Danes

Professor George Golitsyn

Pragya Dipak Gyawali

The Honorable Thomas Hughes

Dr Jiro Kondo

Dr Hoesung Lee

Professor Tom Malone

The Honorable Robert McNamara

Professor Richard Odingo

Professor Thomas Schelling

PACIFIC NORTHWEST NATIONAL LABORATORY

Steering Committee

Chester L. Cooper

James A. Edmonds

Elizabeth Malone

Steve Rayner

Norman J. Rosenberg

Support staff

Allison Glismann

Laura Green

Suzette Hampton

Jenniffer Leyson

K Storck

AUTHORS, CONTRIBUTORS, AND PEER REVIEWERS

W. Neil Adger, *University of East Anglia, UK*

Ahsan Uddin, Ahmed *Bangladesh Centre for Advanced Studies, Bangladesh*

Mozaharul Alam, *Centre for Advanced Studies, Bangladesh*

W. B. Ashton, *Pacific Northwest National Laboratory, USA*

Marjolein van Asselt, *University of Maastricht, the Netherlands*

Viranda Asthana, *Jawaharlal Nehru University, India*

Tariq Banuri, *Sustainable Development Policy Institute, Pakistan*

Richard Baron, *International Energy Agency, OECD, France*

Igor Bashmakov, *Center for Energy Efficiency, Moscow*

Richard E. Benedick, *World Wildlife Fund, Conservation Foundation, USA*

Wiebe Bijker, *University of Limburg, the Netherlands*

Daniel Bodansky, *University of Washington School of Law, USA*

Larry Boyer, *George Washington University, USA*

Judith Bradbury, *Pacific Northwest National Laboratory, USA*

Harvey Brooks, *Harvard University, USA*

Katrina Brown, *University of East Anglia, UK*

Ian Burton, *Atmospheric Environment Service, Canada*

Frederick H. Buttel, *University of Wisconsin, Madison, USA*

Karl W. Butzer, *University of Texas at Austin, USA*

Robin Cantor, *Law and Economics Consulting Group, USA*

Bayard Catron, *George Washington University, USA*

Florian Charvolin, *Centre National de la Recherche Scientifique, France*

Chipeng Chu, *Stanford University, USA*

Chester L. Cooper, *Pacific Northwest National Laboratory, USA*

Robert Costanza, *University of Maryland, USA*

Edward Crenshaw, *Ohio State University, USA*

Pierre Crosson, *Resources for the Future, USA*

Margaret Davidson, *NOAA Coastal Services Center, USA*

Ogunlade Davidson, *University of Sierra Leone, Sierra Leone*

Robert Deacon, *University of California at Santa Barbara, USA*

Ota de Leonardis, *University of Milan, Italy*

Meghnad Desai, *London School of Economics, UK*

Mary Douglas, *University of London, UK*

Hadi Dowlatabadi, *Carnegie Mellon University, USA*

Thomas E. Downing, *University of Oxford, UK*

Otto Edenhofer, *Technical University of Darmstadt, Germany*

James A. Edmonds, *Pacific Northwest National Laboratory, USA*

Paul N. Edwards, *Stanford University, USA*

Paul Ekins, *Birkbeck College London, UK*

Mohammad El-Raey, *University of Alexandria, Egypt*

Aant Elzinga, *University of Gothenburg, Sweden*

Shirley J. Fiske, *National Oceanic and Atmospheric Administration, USA*

Silvio O. Funtowicz, *Joint Research Center, European Commission, Italy*

Erve Garrison, *University of Georgia, USA*

Des Gasper, *Institute of Social Studies, the Netherlands*

Luther P. Gerlach, *University of Minnesota, USA*

Peter Gleick, *Pacific Institute, USA*

George Golitsyn, *Russian Academy of Science, Russia*

Dean Graetz, *Commonwealth Scientific and Industrial Research Organisation, Australia*

Philip C. R. Gray, *Research Center Julich, Germany*

Wayne Gray, *Clark University, USA*

Michael Grubb, *Royal Institute of International Affairs, UK*

Arnulf Grübler, *International Institute for Applied Systems Analysis, Austria*

Howard Gruenspecht, *US Department of Energy, USA*

Simon Guy, *University of Newcastle upon Tyne, UK*

144

Dipak Gyawali, *Royal Nepal Academy of Science and Technology, Nepal*

Peter M. Haas, *University of Massachusetts, Amherst, USA*

Bruce Hackett, *University of California, Davis, USA*

Nick Hanley, *University of Stirling, UK*

Russell Hardin, *New York University, USA*

Shaun Hargreaves-Heap, *University of East Anglia, UK*

Susanna B. Hecht, *University of California, Los Angeles, USA*

Gerhart Heilig, *International Institute for Applied Systems Analysis, Austria*

Edward L. Hillsman, *Oak Ridge National Laboratory, USA*

Frank Hole, *Yale University, USA*

Leen Hordijk, *Wageningen Agricultural University, the Netherlands*

John Houghton, *US Department of Energy, USA*

Hiliard Huntington, *Stanford University, USA*

Saleemul Huq, *Bangladesh Centre for Advanced Studies, Bangladesh*

Evert van Imhoff, *Netherlands Interdisciplinary Demographic Institute, the Netherlands*

Helen Ingram, *University of Arizona, USA*

Alan Irwin, *Brunel University, UK*

Saiful Islam, *Global Challenge Network, Germany*

Henry D. Jacoby, *Massachusetts Institute of Technology, USA*

Carlo C. Jaeger, *Swiss Federal Institute for Environmental Science and Technology, Switzerland and Darmstadt University of Technology, Germany*

Dale Jamieson, *Carleton College, USA*

Marco Janssen, *National Institute of Public Health and the Environment, the Netherlands*

Sheila S. Jasanoff, *Cornell University, USA*

Craig Jenkins, *Ohio State University, USA*

Denise Jodelet, *Ecole des Hautes Etudes en Sciences Sociales, France*

N. S. Jodha, *World Bank, USA*

Andrew Jordan, *University of East Anglia, UK*

Tae Yong Jung, *Korean Energy Economics Institute, Korea*

Hélène Karmasin, *Institut für Motivforschung, Austria*

Rick Katz, *ESIG/NCAR, USA*

René Kemp, *University of Limburg, the Netherlands*

Willett Kempton, *University of Delaware, USA*

Richard Klein, *National Institute for Coastal and Marine Management, the Netherlands*

Rob Koudstaal, *Resource Analysis, the Netherlands*

Chunglin Kwa, *University of Amsterdam, the Netherlands*

Denise Lach, *Oregon State University, USA*

W. Henry Lambright, *Syracuse University, USA*

Bruno Latour, *Ecole Nationale Supérieure des Mines, France*

Stephen Leatherman, *University of Maryland, USA*

Harro van Lente, *KPMG Inspire Foundation, the Netherlands*

Ronnie D. Lipschutz, *University of California, Santa Cruz, USA*

Diana Liverman, *University of Arizona, USA*

Ragnar Löfstedt, *University of Surrey, UK*

Janice Longstreth, *Waste Policy Institute, USA*

Michael Lovell, *Wesleyan University, USA*

Sven B. Lundstedt, *Ohio State University, USA*

Urs Luterbacher, *Graduate Institute of International Studies, Geneva, Switzerland*

Wolfgang Lutz, *International Institute for Applied Systems Analysis, Austria*

Loren Lutzenhiser, *Washington State University, USA*

Michael Lynch, *Brunel University, UK*

F. Landis MacKellar, *International Institute for Applied Systems Analysis, Austria*

Antonio Maghalães, *Ministry of Planning, Brazil*

Elizabeth L. Malone, *Pacific Northwest National Laboratory, USA*

Tom Malone, *Sigma Xi, USA*

Gavan McDonnel, *University of New South Wales, Australia*

Jacqueline McGlade, *Warwick University, UK*

Tom McGovern, *City University of New York, USA*

Douglas McLean, *University of Maryland, USA*

A. J. McMichael, *London School of Hygiene and Tropical Medicihr, UK*

Judith Mehta, *University of East Anglia, UK*

Robert Mendelsohn, *Yale University, USA*

William B. Meyer, *Clark University, USA*

Rob Misdorp, *International Centre for Coastal Zone Management, the Netherlands*

Elena Milanova, *Russian MAB UNESCO Committee, Russia*

Clark A. Miller, *Cornell University, USA*

Vinod Mishra, *East–West Center, USA*

Ronald B. Mitchell, *University of Oregon, USA*

Emilio Moran, *Indiana University at Bloomington, USA*

Tsuneyuki Morita, *National Institute for Environmental Studies, Japan*

Peter Morrisette, *Institute of Behavioral Science, USA*

Han Mukang, *University of Beijing, China*

Dwijen Mullick, *Centre for Advanced Studies, Bangladesh*

Nebojsa Nakicenovic, *International Institute for Applied Systems Analysis, Austria*

Steven Ney, *Technical University, Vienna, Austria*

Robert J. Nicholls, *University of Middlesex, UK*

David Norse, *University College London, UK*

Richard Odingo, *University of Nairobi, Kenya*

Jackton B. Ojwang, *University of Nairobi, Kenya*

Steve Olson, *University of Rhode Island, USA*

Brian O'Neill, *Environmental Defense Fund, USA*

Hans Opschoor, *Free University of Amsterdam, the Netherlands*

Timothy O'Riordan, *University of East Anglia, UK*

John O. Oucho, *University of Nairobi, Kenya*

Edward A. Parson, *Harvard University, USA*

Matthew Paterson, *University of Keele, UK*

David Pearce, *University College London, UK*

Sanjeev Prakash, *Eco-Tibet, India*

Martin Price, *University of Oxford, UK*

Atiq Rahman, *Bangladesh Centre for Advanced Studies, Bangladesh*

Kal Raustiala, *Harvard Law School, USA*

Jerome R. Ravetz, *Research Methods Consultancy, UK*

Steve Rayner, *Pacific Northwest National Laboratory, USA*

John Reilly, *US Department of Agriculture, USA*

Ortwin Renn, *Academy for Technology Assessment and University of Stuttgart, Germany*

John Richards, *Duke University, USA*

Kenneth R. Richards, *University of Indiana, Bloomington, USA*

Richard Richels, *Electric Power Research Institute, USA*

Arie Rip, *University of Twente, the Netherlands*

James Risbey, *Carnegie Mellon University, USA*

John Robinson, *University of British Columbia, Canada*

Richard Rockwell, *Inter-University Consortium for Political and Social Research, USA*

Eugene A. Rosa, *Washington State University, USA*

Luiz Pinguelli Rosa, *Federal University of Rio de Janeiro*

Adam Rose, *Pennsylvania State University, USA*

Norman J. Rosenberg, *Pacific Northwest National Laboratory, USA*

Jan Rotmans, *University of Maastricht, the Netherlands*

Ian Rowlands, *University of Waterloo, Canada*

Paul Runci, *University of Maryland, USA*

Vernon W. Ruttan, *University of Minnesota, USA*

Robert Sack, *University of Wisconsin, USA*

Colin Sage, *Wye College, UK*

Paul Samson, *International Green Cross, Switzerland*

Gerrit Jan Schaeffer, Energy Research Centre, the Netherlands

Thomas Schelling, *University of Maryland, USA*

Jurgen Schmandt, *University of Texas, Austin, USA*

Michiel Schwarz, *Independent Consultant/ Researcher, the Netherlands*

Michael J. Scott, *Pacific Northwest National Laboratory, USA*

Galina Sergen, *University of New South Wales, Australia*

Elizabeth Shove, *University of Lancaster, UK*

P. R. Shukla, *Indian Institute of Management, India*

Udo Simonis, *Science Centre, Berlin*

Jim Skea, *University of Sussex, UK*

Eugene Skolnikoff, *Massachusetts Institute of Technology, USA*

Paul Slovic, *Decision Research, USA*

Youba Sokona, *ENDA–TM, Senegal*

Zofia Sokolewicz, University of Warsaw, Poland

Clive Spash, *University of Stirling, UK*

Bertram I. Spector, *Center for Negotiation Analysis, USA*

Daniel Spreng, *Swiss Federal Institute of Technology, Switzerland*

Detlef Sprinz, *PIK-Potsdam Institute for Climate Impact Research, Germany*

George Stankey, *Oregon State University, USA*

Nico Stehr, *University of British Columbia, Canada*

Paul Stern, *National Academy of Science and Engineering, USA*

Astri Suhrke, *Chr. Michelson Institute, Norway*

Uno Svedin, *Swedish Council for Planning and Coordination of Research, Sweden*

Thanh-dam Truong, *Institute of Social Studies, the Netherlands*

Michael Thompson, *Musgrave Institute, UK and LOS-Senteret, Norway*

Peter Timmerman, *International Federation of Institutes of Advanced Studies, Canada*

B. L. Turner II, *Clark University, USA*

Lando Velasco, *CANSEA, Philippines*

Pier Vellinga, *Free University of Amsterdam, the Netherlands*

Hugh Ward, *University of Essex, UK*

Tom Webler, *Antioch College, USA*

Peter Weingart, *University of Bielefeld, Germany*

George W. Wenzel, *McGill University, Canada*

James L. Wescoat, *University of Colorado at Boulder, USA*

Lee Wexler, *International Institute for Applied Systems Analysis, Austria*

John Weyant, *Stanford University, USA*

John Whalley, *University of Western Ontario, Canada*

Harold Wilhite, *University of Oslo, Norway*

Donald J. Wuebbles, *University of Illinois, USA*

Brian Wynne, *University of Lancaster, UK*

Kenji Yamaji, *University of Tokyo, Japan*

Yukio Yanigisawa, *Research Institute of Innovative Technology for the Earth, Japan*

Steven Yearley, *University of York, UK*

Shira Yoffe, *Pacific Northwest National Laboratory, USA*

Gary Yohe, *Wesleyan University, USA*

Contents of Volumes 1–4

Index of names

Subject index

171

mathematical **1:** 25, 45
perspectives in models **3:** 361–3
    population projections **3:** 362
Ramsey optimal growth **3:** 68
rational economic actor in **2:** 303
reflexivity of researchers **3:** 364
SusClime **3:** 131–2
subjectivity of **3:** 360
system complexity **3:** 364
terrestrial ecosystem (TEM) **3:** 328
as truth machines **1:** 62; **3:** 302; **4:** 119
vertical integration **3:** 318–19
visualization of results **3:** 344
modern growth paradigm **3:** 5
modernization theory **3:** 69–71
macrosocial **3:** 70
monsoon **3:** 253
Monte Carlo simulation **1:** 110–11; **3:** 360
Montreal Protocol on Substances that
  Deplete the Ozone Layer **1:** 31, 33, 52, 290,
  355, 360, 367, 371, 376, 383, 386; **2:** 24; **3:** 6, 85,
  115, 151
moral economy **3:** 266–7
  See also vulnerability responses
morbidity **1:** 154; **3:** 61
mortality **1,2,3:** xxiii; **1:** 92–3, 100–105,
  107–11, 154, 165; **3:** 12–13, 229, 245–7, 308,
  334; **4:** 11, 78
  children **1:** 288
  decline **1:** 96–7; **3:** 12
  health transition **1:** 155
  HIV/AIDS **1:** 156
  infant mortality/survival rate **1:** 152,
    243, 302; **3:** 8
Municipal Leaders Summit for Climate
  Change (New York, 1993) **1:** 393
  Cities For Climate Protection program
    1: 393; **4:** 131–2
myths of nature **1:** 283–9, 292–3, 306; **4:** 127
  See also nature
  equilibrium **1:** 285
  hegemonic **1:** 289–90
  views of climate change **1:** 288–9
    diagnosis and prescriptions
      1: 289–94

Nash equilibrium **3:** 162–4, 200
National Academy of Sciences, US **1:** 302;
  3: 222
National Acid Deposition Program (NADP),
  US **1:** 35
National Aeronautics and Space
  Administration (NASA), US **1:** 32–3, 367,

396
National Environmental Policy Act (NEPA),
  US **3:** 197
National Environmental Policy Plan,
  Netherlands **1:** 396
National Institute for Public Health and
  Environment (RIVM), Netherlands **1:** 14,
  61–2, 64, 68; **3:** 131, 296–7, 330
  Global Environmental Strategic Planning
    Exercise (GESPE) **3:** 131–2
National Oceanic and Atmospheric
  Administration (NOAA), US **1:** 33–4, 396;
  3: 56
National Ozone Expedition to Antarctica,
  US **1:** 33
National Research Council, US (US NRC)
  1: 134, 144, 146
National Science Foundation (NSF), US **1:** 33
National Union of Mineworkers, UK **4:** 111
natural gas **2:** 212–14, 218–19
natural resource wars/renewable resource
  wars **1:** 92, 170–73
natural resources **1,2,3:** xxxviii **1:** 119,
  196, 200, 250, 259; **3:** 2, 15, 36, 39, 42, 68–9, 70,
  75, 78, 80, 92; **4:** 17, 116
  coastal zones **3:** 146
  climate as **3:** 270–71, 275
  degradation **3:** 45
  depletion **1:** 63, 140, 198
  development **3:** 343
  management **1,2,3:** xvi; **1:** 267; **3:** 249;
    4: 5
  marine **3:** 244
  nonrenewable **3:** 78, 80–81
  renewable **1:** 91–2, 146–8, 163, 166,
    170–72, 179, 297; **3:** 78, 80
  substitutability **3:** 69, 76–7
  sustainability of land/water resources
    1,2,3: xxviii, xxix; **2:** 81; **4:** 17
  use **3:** 240–42
  wars **1:** 170–72
nature
  myths *See* myths of nature
  perception of **1:** 44, 46, 282, 287, 322;
    4: 77
    capricious **1:** 285
    ephemeral **1:** 285
    perverse/tolerant **1:** 285
  rights for **1:** 313
needs-driven research **1:** 7
negative freedoms **1:** 243–5
neoclassical economics **1:** 90–92, 115–17,
  133, 163, 174, 176–7, 179–80, 286; **2:** 355; **3:** 6,